To Miss Connie
for binding all
those books.

Bill Winch
July 4, 1956

THE GRANDEUR AND MISERY OF MAN

THE

GRANDEUR AND MISERY

OF MAN

David E. Roberts

New York

OXFORD UNIVERSITY PRESS

1955

INTRODUCTION

THE SERMONS published in this volume express in a unique way the human problems with which the author wrestled during his life time. In spite of his early death, at the age of 44, he achieved a rare insight into the depths of the human soul. This was partly the result of his attempts to relate Christianity, practically and theoretically, to the ideas of modern therapeutic psychology, and partly the result of his extensive counseling of students, especially during the years in which he was dean of students at Union Theological Seminary. During these years he acquired the practical wisdom which is manifest in each of his sermons. But this would not have been possible had he himself not experienced the problems which those whom he counseled also experienced. Through these sermons he will become the counselor of many whom he never saw and who hardly knew him by name. Those who are publishing these sermons hope that through them his work, which was cut short by his premature death, will be extended into the practical realm, just as surely as his theological writings will extend his work into the theoretical realm.

In the sermon on "Christian Certainty," he says: "Let us start, then, with man, no matter how much such a proposal may horrify some theologians." David Roberts knew that the traditional symbols of religion and concepts of theology are empty for those who do not experience them as answers to their questions. Therefore, he began each sermon with a description of man's predicament in general, or of some special expression of it. He starts with the uncertainty about God in order to lead to a certainty in which the basic uncertainty is both preserved and overcome. The way to such certainty is not through argument but through the courage to look at ourselves and to see ourselves as we really are, or in other words, as we are in the eyes of the eternal which cannot be deceived by us. This is an example of the way in which these sermons lead from the insight into man's predicament to the question of God, and from the question of God to the divine answer which can be accepted as well as rejected by man.

The divine answer to the question of human existence is not given in traditional terminology. Actually it is indicated more than given. The Christian message appears on the horizon of the human question, but it is not handled as though it were something at the disposal of the minister and given to his listeners. In all his sermons, David Roberts is always the one who asks a question and points to a possible answer. But he never becomes one of those who cease to ask because they have the answer. Against them he says in the same sermon: "Some people reject Christianity because they think it requires pretending to be sure where one is not sure . . . All I can say is that we as ministers and laymen have done a rotten job." He believes that "a large dose of skepticism," is a prerequisite of faith. In this spirit, which is genuinely Protestant, these sermons are conceived and formulated.

David Roberts' knowledge of what is in man made it impossible for him to follow the line of thought which was still powerful when he started studying: he calls it "the confidence in human possibilities." ("The Grandeur and Misery of Man.") Among the last words I heard him speak a few days before his death were: "If I ever should become healthy again I will be able to say what the demonic is." He was not allowed to, but those who read his sermons (as well as his theological works) cannot fail to recognize that he knew what the demonic is, namely powers in soul and society against which the good will even of the very best of us is without power. He knew the nature of these powers in many individuals, including himself. He experienced them in history and he realized that only the power of grace can overcome them. He knew that this power is not at anyone's disposal, but that one can keep oneself open to it. And it is for such an openness that all of his sermons call.

David Roberts' early death has deprived many people of the help which a personal encounter with him could have given them. For such encounters the written word is no substitute. But the written word reaches more people than the spoken word. And those who read these sermons will find a truly human and

Christian personality with his struggles, his defeats, and his victories.

PAUL TILLICH

Union Theological Seminary
April, 1955

ACKNOWLEDGMENTS

BECAUSE it was my husband's habit to write out his sermons fully, very little editing was necessary in order to prepare them for publication. Nevertheless, some pre-publication work has been involved. For their essential help in this I am grateful to Professor Robert McAfee Brown and his wife, Sydney. I also wish to express my appreciation to Miss Marion Hausner of the Oxford University Press, Inc., for her initial suggestion that this book be published.

ELINOR N. ROBERTS

CONTENTS

xi

THE GRANDEUR AND MISERY OF MAN

SPIRITUAL REBIRTH

Nicodemus said to him,
How can a man be born when he is old?

JOHN 3:4

AWARENESS OF THE NEED for spiritual rebirth occupies a central place in Christianity. But as with any great religious theme, familiarity may deceive us into assuming that we know exactly what it means. We dismiss Nicodemus, with his literal-minded question, as obtuse. Yet if we examine closely what spiritual rebirth would mean for us and for our world, may we not find ourselves on his side of the dialogue — baffled and incredulous?

For we belong to an age that detaches both physical and spiritual birth from God. Accordingly life begins, not as a divine gift, but as a result of a biological process. And transformation occurs, not through Christ, but through psychological and social adjustments. Our unsolved problems are traced back to nature. Having emerged but recently from the forest, man is having a hard time humanizing himself. Fierce instincts rise up when he is threatened; and the need for food, shelter, and procreation can drive him into savage action. The task of building civilization is so precarious that history is strewn with failure; but the failure is understandable. Man has the double task of learning how to control himself and his environment; and sometimes the odds against him are simply too great.

Nevertheless, according to this modern outlook, man has the capacity to become spirit, if by spirit you mean that he can in some measure find his true selfhood in freedom and fellowship. But he must do so on his own. Not, of course, as an isolated individual, but in collaboration with other human beings. Men today are desperately looking for personal maturity and the good society; but they have little patience with the idea that these can be found only in and through divine redemption.

Having forgotten that life itself is a divine gift, they cannot believe that rebirth is also a divine gift. And yet the yearning for regeneration cannot be stifled. The mass religions of the twentieth century are potent only because they promise a new life, with enemies conquered, shackles broken, anxieties stilled. But their shrines turn out to be traps where personality is gobbled up and never restored.

If, against such a background, we would discern afresh the meaning and power of Christian redemption, let us begin by realizing that *we cannot sunder it from this life*. The writers of the New Testament make clear that Spirit is in conflict with "flesh" and "the world" not as such, but only in so far as these are enslaved by sin. Yet throughout the centuries Christian thought has frequently described rebirth in terms that really require a rejection of the body, the world, and nature. "Spirituality" has come to mean something that must be protected from entanglements with marriage, culture, and politics.

But what we find in Christ is not a separation; it is a drawing together, a making whole, a fulfillment of this creatureliness, this human nature, in union with God. The birth of the Christ child is the beginning of *life* and of *new* life at one and the same time, because creation and redemption are both gifts of the same God. If we can speak at all of the birth of the Spirit in ourselves, we must add — in the flesh.

To be sure, only when the fetters have been broken, can a man rightly affirm life; only when he has entered into his true self can he thank God aright for the gift of existence. Only one who loves God fully can believe that He works in everything for good. And you and I may have to confess that we have not yet reached such a vantage point. Our lives are by no means free from bitterness, doubt, and despair. Yet the fact remains that whatever shuts us off from spiritual rebirth at the same time shuts us off from hallowing *this* life — the world of nature, secular tasks, money, power, sex.

It is the whole man, flesh and spirit, who needs to be restored to sonship with God. It is this everyday world of routine and terror which needs to be healed.

It is real people, somewhere in the territory between a lost innocence and a not-yet-found beatitude, who must be reached by the Gospel.

And how often we fail to reach them. Indeed, how often we find ourselves right among them, with the same problems tearing at the roots of our lives and the saving power of the Gospel somehow out of reach. And yet we continue to put the meaning of rebirth up in an ecclesiastical stratosphere. We dream about a form of saintliness which has no connection with our own stubborn selves and our equally stubborn neighbors. Or we point to redemption as beyond history, and then look on this world as so riddled by sin that we do not expect to see visible signs of God's working in our own lives or in the events that surround us.

In the passage from which our text comes, regeneration is connected with baptism. And although as a sacrament baptism is not repeated, what it means can be experienced over and over again in daily life. The old man must die if there is to be a new beginning. The water which cleanses also kills. And as we pass through experiences that may hold a promise of transformation, we feel that we are being destroyed. We go into the depths, not knowing whether we shall ever be able to rise again.

Yet this death of the old man has been misinterpreted whenever it has been equated with conscious resignation and discipline in the Christian Life. But it *issues* from a transformation of the will; it cannot produce that transformation. Sacrifice can be an expression of love; but we cannot conjure up love by being sacrificial.

No. The dying of the old man comes upon us in ways we cannot manipulate. We may strive to cut the ties that bind us to selfishness; but when God does the cutting, it usually takes a form we did not really foresee. It may begin at a point where something is taken from us that we regarded as utterly indispensable.

Each individual must fill in for himself the circumstances that have broken his grip on the old self. Sometimes a terrible upheaval in world events shatters old patterns and compels a new beginning. Sometimes an individual has been so wronged that something must die — either his bitterness or his love, but one or the other. And sometimes, as Alan Paton's novel, *Too Late the Phalarope*, makes clear, disaster may come through strange forces in the self. A man falls into evil so deadly that what he has done either destroys him, or a part of him is washed away so that he rises at last — chastened, broken, but healed.

In theological circles we say that sin consists in absolute attachment to finite good instead of to God. Sin centers life's meaning in the self and in things about which the self cares most. But do we add with full seriousness: "Who then can be saved?" What, in your life and mine, is not, in some sense, a worldly attachment?

To be sure, Christians are not forbidden to cherish

authentic goods in this life — bodily health, the blessings of home, productive work, communal order,
world peace. What monsters we would be if we failed
to cherish these things! But the Christian is bidden
to look beyond them all. Not because we know, with
a fatalistic wisdom, that any one of them can be taken
from us, but because to fail to look beyond them is
to forget the source. Sin, at its roots, is ingratitude. It
is a sort of seizure of life, as though by right, instead
of the receiving of a gift.

Yet who, by taking thought, can put a stop to his
own idolatry? We never know how tightly we have
held a false picture of ourselves, false expectations,
false demands, until our grip is broken. Then we
learn what has been true all along. We have sought
absolute security among things finite and fragile.

Therefore spiritual rebirth is an indescribably risky
business. The same shock that may issue in newness
of life may also lead to breakdown. Any pastor is likely
to encounter a person who says: "I have recovered several times in my life after everything went to pieces;
but now I'm too old." "How can a man be born again
when he is old?"

What is it, then, that lies beyond the breaking of
our willfulness, our idolatry? What lifts us out of the
depths? How does rebirth by water and the spirit
begin?

It begins where God the Creator and Redeemer,
God the source of physical and spiritual life, draws
together what we have driven apart. The power that

comes from above releases power from within. The terrible breach between creaturely vitality and loving service is healed. And the result can only be called a *simplification* of life. Like men who have stared death in the face, we now see what really matters. Things we have regarded as tremendously important turn out to be trivial in comparison with what we have been missing. It is as though the power to live and the power to love now flood into our hearts in a single stream.

The symbol for entrance into the Kingdom is a child, and we can see why. In the child it is as though grace and nature have not yet broken apart. Simplicity, clarity, and uncalculating love are found here.

Admittedly, preaching can abuse the New Testament in such a way that Christianity sounds like an effort to keep people infantile to the end of their days. But we are protected against that mistake if we remember Nicodemus' question. We are talking about an old man. And we must ask not only how he can die away but also how he can be born again. We do not seek the destruction of his most mature powers, but their fulfillment. And we find it in the restoration of *expectancy,* in a new openness to whatever life may bring.

Most of us are held down by a kind of armor which prevents the growth of the new self. This armor protects us against the wounds from our fellows; we can even hide inside it, if need be. We are weighed down by a knowledge of human evil, by hopelessness, by threats from without, and by the need to conceal. Abner Dean has a drawing of a man garbed in such armor, roaring out with rage: "What do you mean, you don't love me?" Like him, we walk about frightened and angry, wondering what has happened to the freshness life once promised.

How can we drop our defenses? How can we go forth to meet the other as he is? How can we make room inside ourselves for the other person when we talk with him?

In the end we cannot answer that question by offering an explanation. But we can describe the result as a gift and as a discovery. The new life always comes, not merely as recognition, but as power. Think of something you have been trying to produce, but which would not come forth in the right way. It is not only artists and poets who undergo such travail. Every human being knows something of it as he tries to manage his own conduct and motivation. And then think of how, perhaps after you had given up in disgust, a resolution of the difficulty burst through. The right words flowed from the pen. Or the right motives flowed from the heart. You found what you had been groping for so fumblingly. Spirit and flesh fell into unison. And you wondered where the gift came from. That which could not be achieved by forcing was granted to you. "The wind blows where it wills, and you hear the sound of it, but you do not know whence it comes and whither it goes; so is every one who is born of the Spirit." (JOHN 3:8)

It may seem ludicrous, when we think about the condition of the world today, to speak of spiritual rebirth at all. We know, all too well, that the misery, the threats, seem in large measure beyond our control. And we know that sometimes the misery and threats seem heightened beyond measure precisely when desperate men seek to bring events, peoples, and power within the vise-like grip of their control.

In the face of such facts, to say that the spiritual rebirth of society must always take place by means of a re-creation of the self seems like a hopelessly impractical remark. And then to add that the essential factor must come to us as a gift — that seems most baffling of all.

Nevertheless, we here touch upon the wonder of the Christian faith. The Advent season, for example, prepares our hearts and minds, partly through what we do consciously, partly through the instilling of penitence and expectancy at levels much deeper than anything we can devise. And we realize that the single theme of our religion, then and always, is rebirth — life and new life breaking into the world together. In the Nativity. In baptism. In conversion. In Resurrection. And we are never completely ready for it, never worthy of it. Yet God comes to us; He is present with us and within us, flooding our hearts. And we can only wonder where the power came from.

Almighty God our Father, teach us we beseech Thee, through any anxiety or suffering that may be-

fall us, how to find strength instead of despair, and how to be filled with sympathy instead of bitterness. And in those moments, especially, when we seem to have reached the end of our own strength and endurance, teach us to commit our lives and all that we hold dear to Thy keeping, in the knowledge that Thy wisdom is more certain than all human plans, and Thy mercy is deeper than all human reckoning. Amen.

THE CHRISTMAS STORY

There was no room for them in the inn.

LUKE 2:7 (K.J.V.)

IT IS RIGHT that we should listen to the familiar words
of the Christmas story as though we were hearing
them for the first time. We can never cease to wonder
at the new creation which God offers to us constantly.
The Nativity can never become for us merely a precious bit of archaic lore, a cherished memory of a distant day. For it is the beginning of the story whereby
we understand how God comes into the world for all
times and for all men. Christmas is a recollection of
something that *has* happened — yes; but it is also a
recollection of something that is happening now.

Let us start the story afresh, then, seeing it as a
contemporary event, like those painters who have
depicted the Nativity in their own land and their own
times — against the background of a New England
winter or a Chinese landscape. Perhaps, for the moment, we should forget the outcome. Perhaps our
gladness will be spoiled if we feel compelled to look
ahead and see that our rejoicing is linked to a career

This sermon was originally published in *Best Sermons, 1946,*
G. Paul Butler, editor, Harper & Brothers, New York. Reprinted by permission.

that will culminate upon a Cross. Perhaps, for the moment, it would startle us to be told that we are rejoicing because of the birth of one who will suffer and die. We give ourselves undividedly to the wonderful fact that God is here among us. *Immanuel.* For the moment, that is enough; and we need a respite from the haunting foreknowledge of what the world will do to the Son of God.

Yet the very fact that we want this respite is significant. It shows the kind of world we are living in, the kind of people we know ourselves to be. Who has not tried to put aside solemn thoughts and misgivings when a child is born into the world? For the moment — in the sheer gladness of this new life — we do not want to look forward to the years of struggle and bitterness, sickness and sin, that lie ahead. Maybe it is because we are sentimental, maybe it is because we have a sound yearning for the recovery of lost peace and decency; but, in any event, we wish for the moment that babies did not have to grow up. We want to give ourselves wholeheartedly to the unalloyed joy of a life which has come into the world — fresh, unspoiled, and surrounded by love.

But this is a flickering, nostalgic mood. When we think of Christ, we do know what is coming — the baptism, the temptations, the calling of the twelve, the wonderful ministry of teaching and healing, the conflict with hardened Pharisaism, the acclaim of the mob, the Garden of Gethsemane, the Last Supper, the betrayal, the Crucifixion, the Resurrection — and we know then of the long centuries when men follow after, with their hearts burning within them as Jesus accompanies them along the road. And so, we cannot really forget what a fateful series of events God set going in Bethlehem on that morning; and when we reflect, we would not have them otherwise. We cannot rejoice at Christmastide unless we rejoice in the whole story; for the glory of God permeates it every step of the way. We cannot really affirm the beginning unless we affirm the culmination. If we feel joy, we must feel it through tears and mortification as we remember what the world did to the Son of God then, and what it does to Him as He comes to us today.

Naturally St. Luke knew the end of the story when he wrote this Christmas narrative. And surely he must have recognized the dramatic appropriateness of the fact that Jesus began His life by being shut out. "There was no room for them in the inn." *Men tried to shut God out, but He was born in a manger just the same.*

Is it not the case that the saving powers are always the ones that we have tried to shut out? Whenever the light dawns, whenever a fresh access of hope lifts a man out of his sin and misery, whenever God's love breaks through and makes him a new creature — it always comes as something he has shut out. He has been willfully blind to it; he has allowed it to dry up inside; he has pressed it down, driven it out of mind, run away from it, disguised it, repudiated it, and tried to forget it. And when that man is rescued, despite himself, it is because, although he has made no place for Christ in his heart, Christ has been born in him just the same. Like the birth of a new child into the world, the birth of the new man takes place in a way which we *cannot* prevent.

I hardly need dwell upon the fact that we are still shutting God out today. Jesus simply does not belong in this world. He does not belong where one has to make his living by competitive triumph over others. He does not belong where one maintains his own security by suspicion, ruthlessness, and a kind of foxy outguessing of his opponents. He does not belong where men are so caught in wholesale destruction that they have time to think of Heaven only in the last fleeting moment when death is crashing down upon them. He does not belong where communities are held together by fear of external foes, where the comradeship of allies is based squarely upon calculation of each other's power and upon a hard-boiled exchange of conquered territory. He does not belong where millions are torn from their homes, and where decent young men die in the trenches, drown at sea, and are shot down in the air. Yes, we *have* shut Him out! There is no room for Him here!

And we are tempted to cry out: "Oh, gentle Son of God, do not come into such a world. It will destroy you. This is no place for sacrificial love. This is no room for someone who cares nothing for money, prestige, and power. This is no room for someone who

is ready to suffer agony and to confront hatred un-
flinchingly. This kind of a world will break you; it
will work its utmost upon you and then cast you aside
and forget you."

There is no room for Him here. That is a fact. But
the other fact is that God comes into the world, nevertheless. He is born in a manger. He belongs to the
outcast, the downtrodden, the humble. He is destined
to be a man of sorrows, acquainted with grief —
wounded for our transgressions, by whose stripes we
are healed. He belongs to everything in the heart of
man that is still capable of contrition and mercy.

And for that reason, He baffles us. The touches of
wonder with which the Christmas story is surrounded
are an indispensable part of it. I once heard Dr.
Julius Moldenhawer tell of how, when he was a
child, he knew so little that he believed the Christmas
story, just as St. Luke tells it. Then came a time when
he knew so much — after studying higher criticism,
comparative religion, and philosophy — that he
could not believe the miraculous setting of the story.
But now, once again, he knows so little that he believes the story just as St. Luke tells it.

What did he mean? I think he meant that if Christian faith is reached at all, it must be reached through
wonder. If we reflect upon it in an ordinary way, we
come to the conclusion that Christmas could not
possibly happen. By all the rules of common sense,
men should long ago have learned what to expect of
themselves. They should have reconciled themselves

to war, selfishness, and hatred, and have come to terms with these hard facts as best they could. Indeed, so long as we leave God out of account, so long as we focus our attention exclusively upon unredeemed humanity, this picture is perfectly accurate. We can easily see through the pretensions of the so-called "perfectionists." We know that the people who try to act from saintly motives are frequently self-assertive and bad tempered. We have learned by hard experience to be suspicious of those impractical individuals who try to live in terms of pure love. We know how easily self-deception can enter in. We know how smothering and how intolerant sweet Christians can be. We know the harm well-intentioned visionaries can do.

We are like the natives of the African forest who were suspicious of Albert Schweitzer because they had never dealt with a white man before who did not want to exploit them. Like them, we are ready to protect ourselves against selfishness and tyranny as best we can; but we are not prepared for decency and generosity free from ulterior motives.

In fact, we are living in a world which would not know what to make of the love of God if seen in the flesh. We say to ourselves, "If Christ were to come to earth today, would we not also fail to recognize Him? Or might we not be like that army 'officer' who admitted that if he were the military governor of Palestine today and Christ were to come again, he would have to execute him again?"

The very fact that we raise this as a hypothetical question shows how attenuated Christianity has become. We say, "If Christ were among us today . . ." He *is* among us today. He is a living power in the world. We treat him as the world has always treated Him; but He is born in us today, nevertheless. We say to ourselves that it cannot possibly happen, but it has happened.

This is assuredly a firm foundation for our joy. For we desperately need this God who can do wonderful things. We desperately need to have our calculations upset. In many respects, human affairs are much the same today as they have always been.

But there is one overwhelming difference. Since Christ is here, we cannot get rid of the haunting realization that *He* is the one who really belongs. He is the one who depicts human life as God means it to be. We are the strangers; we are the outcasts. He baffles and confuses us because we are the ones who are out of line, out of joint, out of focus. We are the distorted image of God; He is the clear picture. And since He has come, since He is here, we can never completely lose this recollection of what we are meant to be — this hope, despite all our misery and hopelessness — of what we may yet become. For Christmas has left indelibly upon the imagination of mankind the vision of a restored humanity and a restored creation. In it we see every level of existence brought into peace and harmony around the babe lying in a manger — the stars in their courses, the animal kingdom of the sheep and oxen, the work of mankind in the shepherds, and the wisdom of mankind in the Magi.

But someone may well ask how this "mere memory" can heal us — how it can bring every one of us back to the point of a new birth, starting afresh, unspoiled, surrounded by love. What about the mark left by all the long miseries of human history? What about the mark left by all the searing agonies and failures in the lives of each one of us?

I reply by concluding as I began. If Christmas is merely a memory of things past, it cannot heal us. But if it is an awakening to things present, it can be the most healing event ever known. If we can believe that the impossible has happened and that though we have shut Him out, God comes into our world just the same, then a restored humanity and a restored creation may be born again in us today.

Perhaps you are familiar with the story of a French soldier who was found suffering from amnesia. When he was picked up at a railroad station, he looked at his questioners blankly, and all he could say was: "I don't know who I am. I don't know who I am." Because he had been disfigured by facial wounds, there were three different families who claimed him as belonging to them. So he was taken to one village after another, where these different families lived, and allowed to walk around by himself. Finally, when he entered the third village, a sudden light of recognition came into his eyes, he walked unerringly down a side street, in through a tidy gate, and up steps of his father's home. Like the Prodigal Son, he had "come to himself." The old familiar surroundings had restored his mind. Once again, he knew who he was and where he belonged.

On Christmas morning we hear the old familiar story of Bethlehem like amnesia victims in a shell-shocked world, who have forgotten who we are and where we belong. And as we make our way with un-erring steps down that side street, where a star stands over a manger, we shall know that we have found the way home. We shall know that we have come to the only place where men can be restored in mind and heart. We shall know that this memory of what happened long ago is at the same time a fresh awakening to what is happening now, through the suffering love of God toward his children. We shall know that, although we may shut God out, the door of the manger stands open for all the world!

O Almighty God, who by the birth of Thy holy child Jesus Christ hast given us a great light to dawn upon our darkness, grant, we beseech Thee, that in his light we may see light; and bestow upon us, we pray thee, that most excellent gift of charity, that the likeness of Thy Son may be formed in us. Send forth among all men the spirit of good will and recon-ciliation. Let those who are offended forgive, and those who have offended repent, so that all thy chil-dren may live together as one family, praising thee and blessing thee for the great redemption which thou hast wrought for us, through Jesus Christ our Lord. Amen.

THREE PICTURES OF CHRIST

Then they arrived at the country of Gerasenes, which is opposite Galilee. And as he stepped out on land, there met him a man from the city who had demons . . . When he saw Jesus, he cried out and fell down before him, and said with a loud voice, "What have you to do with me, Jesus, Son of the Most High God? I beseech you, do not torment me." For he had commanded the unclean spirit to come out of the man. . . . Jesus then asked him, "What is your name?" And he said, "Legion"; for many demons had entered him. . . . Then the demons came out of the man and entered the swine, and the herd rushed down the steep bank into the lake and were drowned. . . . Then people went out to see what had happened, and they came to Jesus and found the man from whom the demons had gone, sitting at the feet of Jesus, clothed and in his right mind; and they were afraid. . . . The man from whom the demons had gone begged that he might be with (Jesus); but he sent him away, saying, "Return to your home, and declare how much God has done for you." And he went away, proclaiming throughout the whole city how much Jesus had done for him.

LUKE 8:26–30, 33, 35, 38–9

WITHIN THIS BRIEF STORY one can find three different pictures of Jesus.

First, He is a *Tormentor*. "What have you to do with me, Jesus, Son of the Most High God? I beseech you, do not torment me."

If you want to miss the point of the story entirely, then dismiss this outcry as the ravings of a demented man with whom you have nothing in common. Embrace the happy fiction that most human beings delight to bask in the presence of perfect Goodness. The only trouble is that you then find the resistance to Christianity down through the centuries quite unaccountable.

The plain fact is that Christ is a kind of a plague to the human race. There is something in all of us that cries out at times: "What a relief it would be if I could just go ahead and live without having that Figure rise before my vision! Why can't he leave me alone?" We are tormented partly because His presence makes us fully aware of our misery and bondage, and partly because it threatens to take away from us those ills and obsessions that we cling to because they seem to be our very selves.

Unless we understand this, you and I shall never be able to detect the nervous defiance that underlies the major criticisms of Christianity. They say: "Put aside this impossible vision of Christian love. Exercise a bit of moderation and common sense. Learn how to accept ordinary human goods, and then you will be free from these tortured longings."

And so we modern men try, by the millions, to find security, prestige, and contentment: "Oh yes, others may blow the world to bits; but remember, son, *you're* one of those sturdy citizens who knows how to contribute to world order. Oh yes, there are people with frazzled nerves, starved souls, and hopeless hearts; but remember, son, *you're* healthy minded."

We, the comfortable polite people, who ask only a reasonable degree of security and success, and who reach it without too obvious a display of ruthlessness, we — especially — hate to come into the presence of Christ. Because in that moment we see ourselves for what we are; and in that moment we know that the demons dwell in us, too.

The second picture shows Christ as a *Healer*. Legion is sitting there clothed and in his right mind. The same Goodness which seems too unreasonable when it makes us aware of our own devilishness brings peace and sanity into our hearts when its power triumphs. Christianity is therefore only half a Gospel — which means that it is no Gospel at all — unless its conflicts issue in restoration and wholeness. From the vantage point of inward cleansing we look back and wonder why we struggled so stubbornly against it. Take, for example, the person whose pride is at stake in a dispute. The very thought of capitulating, of relinquishing his anger, seems intolerable. But suppose, by some gracious means as mysterious as driving demons into a herd of swine, this man gives in to compassion and forgiveness. He feels so wonderful as to marvel at his past misery. He enjoys friendship more than combat, generosity more than power, though he had to be broken before he was ready to discover such facts.

The Gospel brings relief; but it is not the relief of adjustment to the world, and it is not the relief of self-deception. Think of the people who do not like themselves, do not like what they are doing, do not like the treadmill of competition, display, and feverish effort that they are on. Their lives are slipping away with each tick of the clock, and they have never found genuine joy or wisdom or peace. Most of them are so enslaved to the demons of our age that they cannot reach wholeness without passing through a searing conflict. But if the power of Christ must first torment them in order to save them, let them not forget that there is the promise of relief and joy, as well as agony.

Finally, the story shows us Christ as a *Liberator.* The restored man desired to remain close to Jesus, but Jesus sent him away — back to his own house, back to the stream of ordinary life — to make use of his recovered sanity.

The gravest risk confronting the converted man is that he shall hug his new-found salvation to his breast, for fear of putting it in jeopardy. All of us have known people who, having solved some agonizing problem through religion, become afraid to test or risk what has brought them such beatitude. We can understand how they feel, and yet the attitude of Jesus is plain. Real salvation does not so bind us to Him that henceforth we can never take a step without His support. If it is genuine, we shall carry it with us out into the world's temptations and buffetings.

Admittedly we have no right to generalize on the basis of our story. Yet is it not true that any version of Christianity that focuses exclusively upon one of these three pictures of Christ, to the neglect of the others, is bound to be partial and inadequate? Some people seem to be interested only in Jesus the Tormentor. The only message they have to offer is that Christianity should make us ashamed of ourselves. There are others who talk only about the joy and serenity of our religion; in their cheeriness and sentimentalism they are seldom deeply touched by the tragedies and sufferings of the world around them. Finally, there are those energetic, practical people for whom religion means mainly a continuous round of doing good, until their families and their neighbors become completely exhausted trying to keep up with them.

The point of our story is that each one of these versions of Christianity can be rescued from inadequacy only if we are willing to bring the *whole* of life into relationship with the figure of Christ himself. Quite specifically that means: When our consciences need to be quickened, let us turn to Him. When we need to find joy and serenity, let us turn to Him. And when we need strength to carry forward the practical tasks that lie before us in this troubled world, let us still turn to Him. All three pictures become true only when we relate our moments of tormenting inward struggle, our moments of serene fruition, and our moments of emancipated work in the world to that single Figure.

Almighty and most gracious God, we thank Thee that in showing us Thyself in our Lord Jesus Christ, Thou hast also shown us ourselves — our creation in Thine image, the darkness of our sin, and the joy of reconciliation with Thee. Grant us the strength to acknowledge our faults, we beseech Thee. Grant us the faith to receive Thy forgiveness. And as thou dost restore us to fellowship with Thyself, do thou also liberate us for fellowship with our fellow men, whom to serve is to do Thy will. Amen.

BECOMING AND REMAINING

Lord, I believe; help thou mine unbelief.

MARK 9:24 (K.J.V.)

"HOW DID YOU BECOME A CHRISTIAN?" This is a question which, because of reticence, we may seldom ask others. And whenever we put it to ourselves we discover that the question is astoundingly difficult to answer. Any thorough reply quickly becomes the story of one's entire life; for no incident or influence is irrelevant.

There are some people, to be sure, who can isolate one great turning point; but in retrospect most of them realize that preparatory struggles had been going on behind the scenes. They also realize that the constancy of subsequent faith involves repetition, on a less intense scale, of the central experience.

Others are compelled to admit that they have undergone a process of shuttling in and out of conviction. There were times when Christianity made little sense to them. Perhaps they continued to attend religious services in the hope that something would happen. Perhaps they lost touch with the Church entirely, and then returned to it. But even now their periods of stable belief seem to be interspersed with flashes of doubt, confusion, or rebellion.

Then there are also people who have moved un-
interruptedly forward from childhood to maturity
wholly within the Christian fold. In some instances
their religion may be largely a matter of conformity.
Being a church member is much like being an American, and Christianity takes its place along with home
and nation as an indispensable object of devotion. Of
course, devotion is never without value; but often it
is hard for such persons to grasp the most radical and
shattering aspects of the Gospel, and it is especially
hard for them to understand those who have had to
fight their way to personal faith.

Now it does little good to ask whether there should
be these varieties of religious experience. They simply
exist. And we have no means of imposing a single pattern of response, even if we were sure that it would be
best for everybody. Sometimes the decisive events
occur in surprising, indirect ways. One person I know
finally turned toward religion in the midst of a discussion with unbelieving friends whose views he
thought he shared. Suddenly he saw the emptiness
and despair which underlay their cleverness. Their
atheism rang a bell within him, but not the bell they
intended.

In such an instance chance seems to be operating,
although we cannot be sure it is sheer chance. And
even when someone deliberately tries to say the right
word at the right time, the results often remain quite
unpredictable. Once there was a college student who
showed a certain amount of general promise, but who

was drifting along, making the most of campus politics, athletics, and social life. Then one day an older man who was taking a few courses at the college stopped him. This student had no religious interests at all, but the man said; "Jones, you haven't the slightest idea of what you want to do with your life. Right? Have you ever thought of giving it to Jesus Christ?" The chances were ten to one that the student would go back to his fraternity house and tell about the incident as a joke. But in this case the question stuck. It started a gnawing process of self-examination which finally led Jones into the ministry.

This matter of the right time and the right place is mysterious. Every day we are exposed to ideas which could easily revolutionize our lives. Why do most of these ideas pass through our heads without much effect? Why does one of them suddenly stick? A while ago I found a book in my library that had tipped the scales when, as a young man, I was wavering between belief in God and humanism. If I had read the book two years earlier than I did I would not have accepted it. But at the moment it was just right; and I thank God for an author whose theology I have long since rejected.

Even when we can reduce the chance factor by means of an intimate knowledge of the person to whom we speak, what guarantee is there that we shall say the right thing? More important — what guarantee is there that we shall *be* in ourselves, in our lives and hearts, suitable media for the redemptive work of God? In religious discussions, as in all others, we often realize what we should have said after we are home and getting into bed. Then all sorts of appropriate remarks come into our heads, but it is too late.

Let us remember, however, that one incident is seldom the only turning point. Think of the long list of events and persons you must furnish in trying to answer the question: "How did I become a Christian?" For some of us the list includes skeptical critics who helped lead us out of inadequate versions of Christianity. And is the list yet finished, for any of us? Beliefs may undergo such revolutionary changes that the outcome is hardly recognizable in terms of the starting point. Admittedly, by the time we have reached middle age most of us have settled down into basic convictions of some sort. This may reflect depth, stability, and hard-won assurance. But it may also reflect spiritual stagnation. Suppose that we are now quite incapable of changing our beliefs at all. This may mean that we have reached religious maturity. But may it not also mean that we have become blind to dimensions of the Gospel that are far beyond our present grasp?

Christianity has meant *most* to us when it has rescued us from doubt, confusion, and despair. We see its momentousness clearly when we have reached it after a struggle, or are on the verge of losing it. Are we now immune to such states of mind? Provided he is not filled with hatred, no one knows the meaning of Protestant freedom better than the man who has broken away from Roman Catholicism. Some of the finest statements concerning Christ come from Jewish converts for whom He has been not a matter of ecclesiastical inheritance, but an agonizing stumbling block. Several of our most effective Christian writers today were brought up in thoroughly secularized homes. They have come into faith knowing exactly what is at stake. They can speak to a godless world because they know what it is to be immersed in a godless world.

If, by contrast, you and I are now immune to any major upheaval, if our religious outlook has become quite manageable and dependable, may we not have lost, somewhere along the route, the excitement and challenge of the Gospel? Once I heard a thoughtful man say that he did not like going to Church because Christians always take Jesus for granted. And he added: "I wish sometimes the minister would say something that recalled the days of his own doubts, if he ever had any doubts."

Therefore, alongside the question "How did I become a Christian?" let us ask "How can I remain a Christian?" Actually we remain within faith by the same sort of decisions that brought us to it in the first place. As we get up each morning certainly it *is* an open question whether we shall be Christian in any vital sense. Our ideas may remain unchanged. But what about our concrete attitudes and relationships? What about our hearts and wills and actions? The fact

that we gave an affirmative answer to Christ long ago
is certainly relevant now. But the past is no substitute
for the present. When there is a service for the recep-
tion of new members in a Church, we frequently see
a dozen young people from the confirmation class and
a dozen adults who are coming by letter from sister
churches. Then, occasionally, there is one lonely individual who comes forward to be taken in on re-
affirmation of faith. Figuratively speaking, there ought
to be a whole crowd coming forward on re-affirmation
of faith. And each individual should say something
like this: "I remain a Christian amidst an amazing
combination of circumstances: the continuing influence of my upbringing, rebellion against my upbringing, certainty lost, certainty found again, wise
encouragement from some fellow-Christians, stupid
advice from others, external circumstances that bring
matters to a head, inner struggles that bring matters
to a head, a long search, a sudden victory." A few
members might need to look up at the preacher and
say: "There is a religious need in me so deep that
your ineptitude cannot drive me away."

Yet having discussed the influence of other people
upon our lives and the renewed exercise of personal
decision, we have not really touched the heart of the
matter. The work of man is indispensable, but insuf-
ficient. It is a *medium* of faith, but not faith itself.
Faith is a fellowship with God which is stronger than
anxiety, guilt, and loneliness. What we do with our
human capacities may erect or remove obstacles, but

it can never produce the gift itself. Looking backward we can see how God brings men and situations into the plot of a drama that leads us to Him, even though some of the factors seem utterly alien to His will.

How often we go astray in our own devotional lives by assuming that we must make proper preliminary arrangements; otherwise God can do nothing. On the contrary, is it not sometimes the case that God, who is always present, appears only after we have cut through the verbiage, the ritual, and the church-going habits that delude us into thinking we are in touch with him?

Prayer is direct communion with God. Yet how often do we think of it as something bestowed by Him instead of something arranged by us? No one denies that an appropriate setting, noble liturgical language, and the sustaining presence of others can create favorable conditions. No one denies that wandering thoughts, worry, and hatred can constitute obstacles. Yet we can no more guarantee the presence of God than we can guarantee that another person will love us.

Strictly speaking, Paul's encounter with Christ on the Damascus road was a great instance of *prayer*. And, on a less dramatic scale, every man genuinely engaged in prayer is confronted by a shattering presence. If this presence is a sheer gift, there are bound to be some seekers who feel cheated because it has been withheld from them. On the other hand, there are irreligious people who say that since nothing mystical has ever happened to them there is no occasion to believe in God. In both instances language bedevils us. The frustrated seeker hopes that God will break in from outside. The unbeliever takes for granted that nothing ever will break in from outside. But both work with a preconceived idea of the encounter with God.

Actually faith is not so much the breaking in of something never there before, as it is the effectual appropriation of a relationship that has been there all along. Sometimes our attempts to reach God are so intermingled with our attempts to evade Him, that what we really need is a totally different approach. It is our evasiveness which makes us strain; and it is our straining that keeps us evasive.

I know a person right now for whom life is empty and intolerable. He believes that God forgives other people; but he can find no sense of forgiveness for himself. Is it harsh to suggest that here straining is mixed with evasion? After all, one has to be a very remarkable person to be the *only* member of the human race whom God cannot forgive. May not this feeling of being unparalleled and in a class by himself be what my friend cannot yet relinquish? His sense of worthlessness is so interwoven with a feeling of self-importance that he cannot yet find the blessedness of his true worth in God's sight.

The main point is that you and I cannot create God's forgiveness toward this person. Nor can the individual make it real by conscious decision. Yet, the relationship is already offered from God's side; and if my friend ever undergoes, in his own way, a meeting upon the Damascus road, the important change will occur not outside, but inside. His grip upon this odd mixture of self-hatred and self-importance will finally be broken, and he will enter effectually into a relationship he has known about, from a distance, for a long time.

What makes us Christians and what keeps us Christians, then, is not wholly within our control. At the beginning I suggested that sometimes sheer chance seems to play a role; yet I raised a doubt as to whether we have the right to speak of chance in this connection. Now let me reject the word altogether. We have been speaking of the unfathomable intersection between God's grace and man's search. And in view of the suffering of mankind, the threats which hang over human existence, the shattering demands the Gospel makes upon us, let us rejoice that we do not have to confine ourselves to talk about man's search — and stop there. What we encounter beyond the farthest reaches of the search is a fellowship of trust. In this fellowship we cannot coerce God; but neither is His presence capricious and arbitrary. Rather, He meets us at that point where we truly face ourselves.

What would happen if instead of hanging onto Christianity, or defending it, or taking it for granted, we would recognize that the reality of God is up to Him? What would happen if we realized that His forgiveness is not within our power and that we cannot guarantee it for anybody, including ourselves? Might we not then find that our relationship to Him — deep down in our lives — directly reflects what we are? Might we not discover that the problem of sustaining faith each day is one not of hanging on, but of letting go — letting go of ourselves?

Once I heard a man say: "I spent twenty years trying to come to terms with my doubts. Then one day it dawned on me that I had better come to terms with my faith. Now I have passed from the agony of questions I cannot answer into the agony of answers I cannot escape. And it's a great relief."

"How did I become a Christian?" "How do I remain one?" We can give long accounts of the human circumstances and relationships. But in the end there is only *one* answer we cannot escape. We point to the gift of God Himself in Christ Jesus our Lord."

Almighty God, our Creator and Redeemer, we thank Thee for every gracious influence which has guided our hearts to Thee through the wisdom and affection of other people. We thank Thee, too, for every difficulty which has compelled us to renew the search, longing for Thy Presence from afar, and entering into faith as though for the first time. Above all we thank Thee for the constancy of that love which follows us through every doubt and wandering, helping us in the midst of unbelief, and welcoming the penitent heart with a Father's blessing, through Jesus Christ our Lord. Amen.

CHRISTIAN FREEDOM

> There is therefore now no condemnation to them
> which are in Christ Jesus, who walk not after the flesh,
> but after the Spirit. For the law of the Spirit of life in
> Christ Jesus hath made me free from the law of sin and
> death.
>
> ROMANS 8:1–2 (K.J.V.)

PROTESTANTISM has always taken freedom seriously.
It was one of the great themes of the Reformers, as
Luther's work, *On Christian Liberty,* makes clear.
When we look at our own day, however, what do we
find? The political and moral meanings of the word
"freedom" are on everyone's lips; but the full religious meaning has almost been forgotten. In politics
we are troubled about how we can protect democracy
against its enemies without undermining the liberties
we seek to safeguard. In morals we are troubled about
how to protect society from license without undermining the responsibility of the individual.

But some of us fail to realize how much our modern
perplexities are due to the fact that these freedoms
have been cut adrift from their Christian anchorage.
For example, we easily tend to think of men in the
mass. We read the results of a political poll, and we
picture the voters as though they were a school of fish

swimming this way or that. We forget that each vote represents a personal decision. Or we make generalizations about Jews and Negroes, forgetting that each of them is an individual. Or we feel that since everybody in the neighborhood is buying a television set, we must buy a television set. Some of these things, like mass entertainment and mass advertising, are fairly harmless; and some of them, like totalitarian propaganda and race prejudice, are extremely perilous. In any case, the dignity and independence of the individual are being threatened all over the world. I assume that none of us needs to be reminded of what this means, that it means a challenge to our whole conception of life. But where did this conception come from? How did it gain a foothold in Western civilization? How did it become so firmly rooted in our country? The answer, of course, is "the Bible."

And yet many people today take for granted that the tree of liberty can continue to bear fruit after its roots are destroyed; they take for granted that we can retain human freedom even after we have lost faith in God. You and I are falling into this pattern of thinking whenever we assume that through science, or the economic system, or military might, we can solve our own problems unaided. All of these activities are important; but when they begin to operate apart from obedience to God and as substitues for faith in God, then it is the duty of Protestants to remember their name. It is high time for us to "protest."

Surely what has happened during our own generation in Italy, in Germany, in Russia, drives home with tragic force the lesson that when man cuts himself off from God what he finds is not freedom, but slavery. When we begin to worship our own powers they turn into monsters, and we are enslaved to anxious dread about what our science, our economic system, and our military might may do to us.

And so, modern life presents us with this curious mixture. On the one hand, we are confident that we are quite capable of running the universe. But on the other hand, we feel like weak victims of mass forces that are utterly beyond our control. It is to modern man in the midst of this confusion between pride and fear that the Christian message must be addressed.

The first thing to be said about the contribution of the New Testament to this dilemma is that it makes clear how man can be both responsible and enslaved at one and the same time. It takes for granted that the individual is the source of his own actions; but it also takes for granted that the individual stands in need of a conversion which he cannot produce on his own power. In other words, man's freedom leads to misery when he tries to use it for self-centered purposes; he can find perfect freedom only in the service of God. But this means that true freedom comes to us as a gift; we receive it on God's terms instead of ours; we enter into it only when we are so mastered by God's love that our own stubborn wills have been replaced by His Spirit.

From what, more exactly, does man need to be freed? St. Paul's answer, in the text above, summarizes the whole teaching of the New Testament. We need to be made free from sin, law, and death. These are old-fashioned words, and some people regard them as morbid. But the realities these words point to are as old as the human race, and they never take a holiday, even though we may try to ignore them. It was through a rediscovery of this Pauline teaching that Martin Luther began the Reformation; and it is only through a rediscovery of its relevance to our own lives that we can grasp the basic meaning of Protestantism.

Let me put the point in familiar language. You and I are continually falling short of love and rebelling against it. We do many selfish things, and, acting in concert with large groups of other men, we are caught in the midst of wicked and tragic events. But we will never understand our predicament if we look only at the deeds themselves. The real cause of our trouble is to be found in a condition of the human heart, out of which all actions proceed. This is the condition that the Bible calls "sin," and it means that human nature itself needs to be transformed. Hence the Churches have caught only a fraction of the full Biblical truth if they spend all their energy trying to fight particular sins, instead of concentrating upon that inner condition which is the abiding cause of evil deeds.

Whenever a man realizes the seriousness of this problem, it is natural for him to try to devise a remedy. The most familiar strategy down through the centuries has been to set up a series of rules. It is as though man, finding himself trapped at the bottom of a dark well, decides that he will make a ladder of good resolutions; and he hopes by strenuous effort to force himself up that ladder, rung by rung, until by the time he reaches the top he has made himself righteous.

Notice that this kind of program does not treat either morality or religion lightly. On the contrary, it takes moral failure so seriously that it sets up a rigid discipline; and it takes God so seriously that it forbids man to stand in His presence until his defects are overcome.

Yet it was precisely this conception of the "law" against which both St. Paul and Martin Luther revolted. Why? Because they saw that a man cannot climb out of a well unless his ladder is fastened at the top. Indeed, it is as though man had broken his legs when he fell into the well. Therefore if the ladder of legalism is the only solution, he is without hope. If he must be able to drag himself upward before he can ever see the sun again, he is doomed to darkness. Only if Someone from above will come down to him in the midst of that darkness and help him upward to the light, has he any hope of salvation.

St. Paul and Martin Luther had tried the ladder of legalism, and they knew it did not work. One of them had been a Pharisee who had followed the Jewish law all his life; but in the end he could only say of it: "O wretched man that I am! Who shall deliver me from the body of this death?" (Romans 7:24, K.J.V.) The other man had been a monk, wearing calluses on his knees in prayer; he had surpassed all others in good works and in stern discipline; and yet, he also knew that his heart was not right with God. A little girl once put the discovery of these great men into very simple words. She said: "The harder I try, the better to be, the worser I am." And the more our consciences are awakened to our true condition, the more every one of us must say something similar. "Oh wretched man that I am! Who shall deliver me from this paralyzing, guilty conscience?"

St. Paul links this bondage to sin and to the law with death. Why does he do that? Is it not obvious that everyone is going to die, the good men as well as the bad? How can sin make death either more or less inescapable for anyone? What St. Paul meant is that a self-centered existence, enslaved to a bad conscience, not only ends in death; it *is* death, because it is separation from God. It is hell on earth. And so long as we are shut off from divine forgiveness, so long as our human relationships are lacking in love and hope, life goes by as a terrible, frustrating curse. All our labors, all our aspirations, all our friendships lead, in the end, to a blank wall.

Only by experiencing the trustworthiness of God in fellowship with Him *now*, can we know that God is trustworthy eternally. And when we have learned to put the present in His keeping, then our fears of death disappear too.

We know, then, what we need to be freed from; but how can we believe that this emancipation is possible? It was through their deepened awareness of human need that St. Paul and Martin Luther received their deepened awareness of the Christian answer. For in Christ they found that God Himself had come down to them in the midst of their darkness and failure, instead of standing aloof from human need, saying, in effect, "You must climb out into the sunlight before I will look upon you again." He Himself had descended into the pit of human guilt in order to raise men up into the light. In Christ, God took upon Himself the burden of human wickedness, and the weight of that burden is to be measured by the suffering on the Cross. God *acted* in Christ. This is the Gospel. This is what enables us to say: "Through freedom, Christ has made us free."

Now notice that if the Gospel is true, then the basis of freedom is to be found not in ourselves, but in a Person who comes into human life. If we try to define freedom merely by looking at our own moral and political capacities, we are overlooking its foundation. That is why I said earlier that democratic liberty and moral responsibility begin to wither when they are cut off from Christian faith. In other words, these earthly freedoms can be nourished only through fellowship with a forgiving God.

It is at this point that Protestantism offers its supreme contribution. For it insists that the freedom which Jesus Christ has made available to us as a gift can continue to work in the Church through the Holy Spirit. This Protestant outlook directly reflects what St. Paul says in II Corinthians 3:17 (K.J.V.), "Now the Lord *is* that Spirit; and where the Spirit of the Lord is, there is liberty." I do not wish to indulge in unkind controversy with Roman Catholics, but as we compare our own tradition with theirs, we have a right to ask questions in trying to reach clarity concerning our differences. Which point of view, Roman Catholic or Protestant, genuinely safeguards the liberty of the Church? Which point of view acknowledges that saving power comes from God alone, instead of from man? Which point of view opens the Bible to all men in any age to be read under the freedom-giving guidance of the Holy Spirit?

I leave you to answer these questions for yourselves. But I beseech you to answer them. Protestants spend a great deal of time worrying about how to match Roman Catholicism in organizational skill, in educating the young, in building cathedrals, in influencing Washington, or in influencing Hollywood. And I can understand these worries. But why do we spend so little time in concentrating upon the point where we are strongest, instead of upon points where our scandalous divisions make us weak? One thing all Protestants have in common is fidelity to the Gospel message of freedom; and unless we can state our case for this fidelity convincingly in open debate then we have no foundation, and we do not deserve to win.

This Christian freedom begins with the new life in Christ as continued through the Church by the work of the Holy Spirit. But it does not end there. It reaches fruition only as this new life is carried out into the surrounding world. It reaches fruition only *in love for the neighbor.*

On April 16, 1521, Martin Luther arrived in Worms to face one of the greatest ordeals of his life. He entered the city amidst a terrific popular demonstration and then went to bed almost dead with fatigue. He was scheduled to appear before the Diet the next afternoon. When he woke up in the morning, what did he do? Did he spend a few feverish hours putting some finishing touches on his speech, as you and I would do? No. He spent that morning visiting a dying man who had expressed a desire to see him. He heard this man's confession and administered the sacrament. And we are told that in the afternoon, when he went before his accusers, he entered the hall smiling.

There in a single story is the secret of the Reformation. When a man has been released from self-centered fears, when he has learned to trust God's power instead of his own, he has been set free for the service of others. And to love men as Christ loves them means taking our place alongside them *while they are yet sinners,* instead of passing self-righteous condemnation upon them. There have always been many people, including Church people, who have found this difficult to understand. It seems to leave the gates wide open for wickedness. St. Paul himself had to guard against this misunderstanding by writing: "Shall we continue in sin, that grace may abound? . . . shall we sin, because we are not under the law, but under grace? God forbid!" (Romans 6:1, 15, K.J.V.)

The point is, of course, that Christianity stands above stuffy morality because it has a *much better* remedy for wickedness. What is this remedy? First, awaken men to their need for divine forgiveness by pointing to that figure on the Cross. Second, bear witness to the place where men can find such forgiveness by pointing to that figure on the Cross.

Jesus Christ is the final answer to the evils and tragedies of every age because until a man's heart has been transformed, his actions cannot really be good, he cannot really serve God and his neighbor, no matter how well he may conform outwardly to the moral standards of his society.

Therefore, let us be of good courage. Nothing can destroy the freedom that is given to us in Jesus Christ. This remains, whether we think of sin, law, or death, and whether we think of them in terms of personal tragedy, or in terms of political catastrophe. This remains, despite the barriers of nation, race, and class, drawing men into a universal fellowship. Because the foundation of our freedom is in Christ, instead of in our sinful selves, we can endure struggle and defeat in humility and hope. Because the foundation of our freedom is in Christ, we can find joyous liberation *now* in the service of a fellowship of suffering love.

Grant unto us, Our Father, the glad confidence and liberty which come through trust in Thy sufficiency. Help us to see every opportunity and peril in the light of Thine unfailing strength and compassion. And teach us, we beseech Thee, to measure the importance of our own concerns by the infinite love which Thou hast shown toward us in the gift of Thy Son, in whose name we pray. Amen.

TRUTH IN THE INWARD BEING

Behold, Thou desirest truth in the inward being.

PSALMS 51:6

AT FIRST GLANCE these words of the Psalmist seem to make a very simple demand upon us. After all, sincerity calls for no special training and no special accomplishments. Here the educated man and the ignorant man stand on an equal footing. Here advantages of wealth and background and talent make no difference at all.

And in an age when the truth is frequently so hard to reach is it not a comfort to be told that God requires merely a simple honesty about ourselves? In science, law, and medicine, getting at the truth requires long, specialized training, and many who start out along those routes fall by the wayside. In political affairs we have to plow our way through a mass of propaganda and deceit. Even in everyday matters, we constantly have to pierce behind exaggeration and ingenious lies. Think, for example, of what confusion would result if we took all advertisements literally. I read sometime ago of a little girl who had broken into her piggy bank and bought a very powerful headache remedy. When her mother asked her why she had done it, she replied

49

that a nice man on television had told her that something terrible might happen unless she went out and bought the medicine right away.

And so it is a relief to realize that, no matter how much we may be surrounded by sham and misinformation, there is one thing that everyone can know with certainty — himself. Everybody can be the greatest expert in the world on one topic — the inward truth about what is going on in his own soul. It sounds simple. And yet, as we all know perfectly well, inward honesty is at the same time the most difficult thing imaginable.

Think for a moment of the ways in which people try to avoid facing the truth about themselves. Think of the amusements, the follies, the feverish work, and the broken friendships that would have to be included in an account of man's endless attempt to get away from himself. Do you not know people who are continually changing their jobs, or the towns they live in, or their circle of friends, or their wives, in the hope that with each new change they will finally be happy and everything will be straightened out? Yet they never succeed because they carry the source of their troubles around inside themselves; therefore they carry it with them into every new situation, and they can never escape from it.

Listen to this letter of advice from an older man to a young man, and see if it does not apply to many of us:

"Do you not know that there comes a midnight hour when all must unmask? Do you suppose that life will

forever suffer itself to be treated as a joke? Do you suppose that, like Cinderella, you can slip out a little
before the midnight hour? Or does this fail to frighten
you? In the course of my life I have seen people who
have so long deceived others that finally it has become
impossible for them to be honest with themselves and
the dishonesty may reach such a degree that they literally destroy their own personalities. Yet you wantonly
practice the art of making yourself a riddle to everybody. My young friend, suppose that nobody troubled
himself to guess your riddle — what enjoyment would
you have in it then? But above all, for your own sake,
put a stop to this wild flight. For you wish to reduce
everything to nothingness. To this end you harden
your heart. You are quite ready to admit that you are
good for nothing, and that the only thing that amuses
you is to walk seven times round existence like Joshua
walking around the walls of Jericho and blow your
trumpet and then see the whole thing collapse." *

Yes; it is a fact that sometimes facing the truth about
ourselves is so painful, so forbidding, that we will
smash everything in sight before we will submit to such
a terrible indignity. Instead of being easy and natural,
then, this achievement of "truth in the inward being"
seems to involve terrific strain. We can see this in connection with someone else when we say, "Oh, I wish

* This passage is a running paraphrase of part of a letter
from Judge William to his "young friend." The original passage is in Kierkegaard, EITHER/OR, Vol. II, Princeton University Press, 1944, pp. 135–6.

he could take a good look at himself for once." But we do not like it at all when the same saying is applied to us.

Let us ask, then, where the difficulties lie. For one thing, inner honesty is often *highly inconvenient,* and many people simply do not want to pay the price. It may demand a good deal of moral courage to refuse to be swayed by popular opinions. It may require willingness to sacrifice when personal advantages lie in one direction while the still, small voice calls in the opposite direction. When fidelity exacts a fearful price, then it is easy to stifle it by saying: "Oh, for goodness sake, where's your sense of humor. Stop trying to be a saint. If all these other people say it's right, your conscience must be wrong." In that moment we start lying to ourselves for the sake of our own comfort. We begin to pass moral responsibility around from one neighbor to the next (as in that town where everybody made a living by taking in everybody else's washing), and no one is willing *to take a stand* — all by himself, if necessary.

Far more important, though, is the fear that if we look at the unvarnished truth about ourselves we shall find something hopeless and irremediable. In other words, one major cause of dishonesty is *inner despair.* A person can stare at an insoluble problem just so long; eventually he reaches the point where he has to have relief. How many times have you heard someone say, in a candid moment: "Yes, I know I'm fooling my-self; but after all, I have to have something to keep me going."

I wonder if you are familiar with the story about a medieval blacksmith who took such pride in his work that he put a special mark upon everything he pro-duced. At length the town was conquered by an in-vading army and he was thrown into a dungeon. He was shackled there with heavy chains, but this did not bother him very much. He was an exceedingly power-ful man and he knew all about chains. He was confi-dent that by finding the weakest link and exacting pressure upon it, he could break loose and make his way to freedom. But as he passed the chain through his hands, he came upon that secret mark which told him that he himself had forged it. And he cried out in de-spair, because he knew he would find no weak link in that chain. He was doomed to be held in bondage by fetters that he himself had forged.

Many people are afraid to look at themselves for fear that they will see something like that blacksmith — a person bound hand and foot by what he himself has made and from which there is no escape.

But in the end it is not even despair that is the main obstacle to honesty. I confess that I was greatly sur-prised when I came upon what the main obstacle is, and it may not make much sense to you when I put it into words. For it is a *fear of fellowship*. Yet the plain fact is that we never can achieve complete honesty as long as we shut ourselves off from other persons. If honesty is genuine, it has to be expressed through openness in our human relationships.

Let me give an example to show what I mean. Frequently, when a person confides something humiliating about himself, you had better expect that the next day, or sometime shortly thereafter, that person may show resentment toward you. No matter how sympathetically you listen, and no matter how gently you deal with him, he is likely to feel you are secretly laughing at him or have contempt for him. The next morning he will regret having told you so much. He will be angry because now his secret is out in the open.

Actually what he is most angry about is that when he has once told his secret to another person, he now has to admit it to *himself* in a way that he has never done before.

Now notice that if what I have been saying is true, then obstacles to honesty and obstacles to human fellowship and obstacles to prayer all come down to the same thing in the end. The Psalmist discerns this truly when he tells us that it is *God* who is satisfied with nothing less than "truth in the inward being." You and I have read plenty of objections to prayer in clever books; but these books usually fail to mention the chief obstacle of all. And, if you will not misunderstand me, I shall put the matter in the first person singular. I *object* to dropping all my defenses in God's presence. I *object* to laying bare my heart and soul before the

One whom I cannot deceive at all. The instinct to run away from that fellowship which brings our secrets out into the open is as old as the human race. Adam and Eve tried to run away and hide in the Garden of Eden. Francis Thompson tried to run away and found himself pursued relentlessly by "The Hound of Heaven." As long as any spark of honesty remains alive within them, all men and women find the same thing to be true.

To such people — that is, to all of us — the Christian Gospel comes with a message which is very old, and yet new every time someone feels his own need deeply. For the Gospel tells us that because God in Jesus Christ has taken upon Himself the burden of our shortcomings, we shall come into His presence, not with fear, but in trust. It opens up a way whereby "truth in the inward being" can become the most healing and comforting thing we have ever known, instead of being a painful ordeal.

I once knew a young man who was struggling with a very serious problem; he carefully tried to conceal the struggle from his best friend, because he was afraid that if the friend found out, their friendship would be ruined. But at last the young man could stand it no longer, so he went to his friend and told him the whole story. And the friend replied: "I've known about it all along, and I've liked you in spite of it."

As you can imagine, that young man went away with

a tremendous burden lifted from his shoulders. He had exposed the worst about himself, expecting to be rejected; and he had come away — accepted.

So it is in our relationship with God. After all, God has known about human sinfulness for a long time now. And if He loves us, it is not because we have succeeded in fooling Him. If He loves us, He loves us in spite of everything. And when our distrust and hardness of heart break down enough so that we can face the worst about ourselves, what we find in His presence is not rejection, but acceptance. And we also find that if we can face a problem in fellowship, it is never so hopeless as when we have to face it in solitude.

But this is not quite the end of the matter. For God knows not only the worst about us; He knows the best about us, too. Think of all those flickering impulses of genuine compassion which you and I have had toward other people, and which we were too awkward to communicate to them. Think of the decent motives which have gone out from us in a fairly straightforward fashion and have somehow gotten all twisted and misunderstood amidst the confusing web of human relationships. Think of the inner core of sensitivity, and humility, and hope, which lies buried behind the protective shell of our personalities. There are the makings, hidden away in your interior, of a better person than you have ever been. And you thought all the time that these secrets about the best things in you would die with you, locked up inside. But if you will learn how to come into the presence of God, you will also discover how to let the best that is in you come out into the light.

Most merciful Father, by whose grace we have been called into the service of Christ's Kingdom, through whose abiding Spirit our hearts are strengthened, and in whose fellowship alone we can confront the future undismayed, help us, we beseech Thee, to obey Thy will in all that lies within our power, and teach us to leave to Thy providence and mercy all that lies beyond our power. Grant us patience and diligence in our common tasks; give us love for truth above cleverness, for honesty above safety, and for persons above ideas. And so draw us together now through faith in Thee, that we may abide in the fellowship of Thine eternal love, through Jesus Christ our Lord. Amen.

CHRISTIAN CERTAINTY

I ask, then, has God rejected his people? By no means!
. . . But through their transgression salvation has come
to the Gentiles, so as to make Israel jealous. Now if their
transgression means riches for the world, and if their
failure means riches for the Gentiles, how much more
will their full inclusion mean! . . . For if their rejection means the reconciliation of the world, what will
their acceptance mean but life from the dead? . . . I
want you to understand this mystery, brethren: a hardening has come upon part of Israel, until the full number of the Gentiles come in, and so all Israel will be
saved . . . For God has consigned all men to disobedi-
ence, that he may have mercy upon all. O the depth of
the riches and wisdom and knowledge of God! How unsearchable are his judgments and how inscrutable his
ways!

ROMANS 11:1, 11–12, 15, 25–6, 32–3

IN THE CHAPTER from which these verses come, St. Paul
offers an explanation of God's dealings with men. He
shows how the rejection of Christ by his own people
has, in a sense, made the faith of the Gentiles possible.
God has so used the unbelief of the Jews as to make it
contribute to the universality of the Gospel. Therefore
the Apostle urges that the universality of the Gospel

This sermon was originally published in *Best Sermons, 1951–
52*, G. Paul Butler, editor, The Macmillan Company, New
York. Reprinted by permission.

will ultimately embrace those who now reject it. Since God can use lack of faith to produce faith, Christians should include the Jews in their hopes instead of excluding them.

But the explanation concludes with an outburst which seems to contradict it. "O the depth of the riches both of the wisdom and knowledge of God! how unsearchable are his judgments, and how inscrutable his ways!" (Romans 11:33) How can God's judgments be unsearchable if the Apostle has just succeeded in delineating them? Which side shall we choose? Shall we believe St. Paul when he tells us that he has reached insight into God's wisdom, or shall we believe him when he suggests that no one "has known the mind of the Lord?"

Actually we must accept both sides. From beginning to end, the Bible tells us both that we can know God, and that God is unfathomable. As a consequence, Christians can always go astray in either of two directions. First, they can become so confident about their doctrines, creeds, systems, and proofs that the mystery of God is forgotten. Secondly, they can represent divine truth as so utterly inaccessible that many people give up the quest altogether or decide that one man's religious hunch is as good as another's because nobody really knows.

But how can we possibly accept both sides? How can we say, with the 13th chapter of First Corinthians, that "we know in part"? How can we admit that this partial knowledge is always imperfect, always subject

to human distortion, always in need of correction —
and at the same time declare that it is knowledge instead of sheer ignorance, error, and illusion?

I do not propose to discuss this problem as an intellectual puzzle. I raise it, rather, because all of our
most urgent practical difficulties come back to this one.
How can we, as Christians, stand firm against fanaticism without falling into fanaticism? How can we believe in the universality of the Gospel without falling
into arrogance toward non-Christians? How can we
effectively preach a mystery to men who clamor for
definite, simple answers? They can be persuaded or
dragooned into laying down their lives, but only in
response to tangible promises of power or security or
revenge. How can we ask them to give their lives, their
whole selves, to the service of God, if we must tell them
in the next breath that no one knows fully what the
will of God is?

Some humane and potentially religious people turn
away from the Church because they fail to find satis-
factory answers to such questions. They feel, to put it
bluntly, that knowledge of God is not a major issue.
They observe that a man can strive for freedom, truth,
and brotherhood whether he believes in God or not.
They also observe that a man may be enslaved to ambition, hatred, and lies whether he believes in God or
not. Indeed, it might be more accurate to say that every
individual is himself a battleground where these opposite sets of forces struggle for supremacy. Therefore
the real issue lies within man himself. The real issue

is whether humility, justice, and love can release us from bondage to regimentation, materialism, and war. As Erich Fromm has put it: "Is it not time to cease to argue about God and instead to unite in the unmasking of contemporary forms of idolatry?" *

We must take this question seriously. Sometimes, we *have* been guilty of talking about the existence of God in such a way that it has no discernible bearing upon the decisive events of human life. Whenever God becomes simply an idea that we want to defend against competing ideas, then it is quite right to say that we have lost touch with the real issue.

Let us start, then, with man, no matter how much such a proposal may horrify some theologians. Let us start with his hopes and fears, his assets and liabilities, his power and weakness. Let us start with his inner battle between slavery and freedom. In that instant the problem is not how we can bring God into connection with our theme, but how we can possibly avoid Him. For I cannot take a step toward deeper self-knowledge without discovering that the answer as to who I am, and what I should be, does not depend exclusively on me. I have my own ideas about what freedom, justice, and love mean; but they are precisely as defective as I am. They reflect the limits of my experience, my insight, my character. If they are ever to be corrected and improved, then the change must come in part from beyond what I am.

* *Psychoanalysis and Religion,* Yale University Press, 1950. p. 118.

You may say that they can be corrected by means of what other people teach me, and this is true. But how do I decide what to accept and what to reject among the influences that come to me from other people? Admittedly my ideas are defective, but so are theirs. Many things about myself I am quite incapable of seeing. But certainly no one else sees me in such a way that there is no distortion, no exaggeration, no blindness. Thus we must say of every human being: "The truth about him is there all the time; but no man knows it fully." Starting with man, we cannot move a step without encountering the fact that a judgment is true only in so far as it participates in something that transcends us.

At times, when we are asked about God we reply as though we were trying to hand out an item of information. But if God is real, then knowledge of Him is not like acquiring information. Instead, it is like the inner upheaval that occurs when we face a new crisis or a new friendship. The basic requirement is not so much that I shall apprehend something as that I shall be able to stand being apprehended.

Picture a man who has organized his life around a stubborn effort to justify himself. Every cause he supports is obviously noble, and all those who oppose his cause are, as he sees it, obviously vicious. What he demands of life seems reasonable to him. If at times he becomes unfair or unreasonable it is always because others have taxed him beyond what flesh can be expected to bear. Every criticism directed against him is a malicious attack. Every criticism he directs against others is a piece of commendable candor. This man is, in short, a kind of "godlet" who judges others by how they fit into his scheme of values.

I say, "Picture such a man." But with minor variations such a man comes very close to being *every* man. Every man is tempted to justify himself beyond the point that is really justifiable. Every man views the worth of others in the light of how they affect his own security, his desires, and his ambitions. And whenever conflict breaks out between two such human beings, neither is completely fair to the other. That is why legal systems have to settle disputes by introducing a judge who is not directly implicated.

But now picture such a man brought into a personal relationship where the Other is completely free from the prejudices and distortions to which all men are subject. Imagine that this Other is able to reveal exactly those truths the man has always managed to evade. All his grandiose notions are shattered. The evil he has done, and the evil that he is, stand out in stark clarity, with no retouching, no possibility of shifting the blame. At the same time, all of his redeeming qualities are recognized. He is not allowed to take credit for more than he is worth; but everything worthy in him is given full weight. Yet the man is more enraged than satisfied by this perfectly fair appraisal. And when he tries to expostulate in self-defense, when he tries to fight back by accusing the Other of ulterior motives, there is no retaliation, no argument. The

Other simply looks at this man with eyes which see right through him — and waits.

Accept this situation as a parable, and you will see why the chief obstacle to knowledge of God is not lack of information. What is called for here is not that we should have brains enough to grasp some irrefutable philosophical theory. What is called for is that we should have courage enough to look at ourselves and to be looked at with the eyes of Eternity. *This* is the major issue; and it cannot even be formulated without bringing us face to face with God, whether we use the word or not.

The man we are talking about is now in the presence of the kind of truth, the kind of love, that can save him. But he can also reject it. He can dig in stubbornly and refuse to see what the Other sees. Indeed, if the Other were interested merely in humiliating or in crushing him, he would have a perfect right to fight back. The most humiliating thing about standing in the presence of God is that He has no interest in humiliating us merely for the sake of humiliation. The most crushing thing is that He does not ask us to wallow in remorse. His presence simply unveils what we are.

This is one of the points at which mystery enters. We can be saved by accepting the truth which comes to us from beyond our own distortions. But in order to be saved by it there has to be something already accessible within us. You and I have seen people fight desperately to hang onto what might be called "the indispensable lie." We have seen them ward off every appeal

to reason and fairness and sympathy. And then sometimes, when they have been driven absolutely to the
wall, it is as though they were able to let go. They have
relinquished their insistent claims; they have stretched
out a hand to the enemy; they have turned from bitterness to forgiveness. And we say of them: "Well, those
fine qualities must have been in them all along. Why
did they fight so stubbornly against letting them come
to the surface? Why did they have to be cornered, and
almost smashed, before they were able to give in?"

Here is the mystery. We do not save ourselves. We
do not conquer our own egotism. It is only because of
the harsh inescapability and the loving inescapability
of the truth from beyond us that we are ever saved.
And yet we participate. The transformation takes place
within us. It is our human potentialities that are
tapped in fulfilling the conditions. The truth from
beyond becomes the truth which we "produce" within

And there is another mystery. The man we were
talking about is free, because he can accept God's
truth or reject it. But notice the odd feature of his rejection. When he holds out, when he will not capitu-
late in the presence of perfect justice and perfect love,
it is as though some demon were driving him. It might
even be more accurate to say that he cannot give in,
he cannot let down his defenses, he cannot have a
change of heart. So the point at which man's freedom
becomes most obvious is also the point at which his
bondage becomes most obvious. Mankind is free to
enslave itself to illusions, to egotism, to conflict. It is

free to do so indefinitely — to the end of time. But man is not free to change God. He is not free to change the nature of justice and love. He is not free to turn lies into truth. He is not free to change his own blindness into honesty.

If then, we return to our initial question, asking how God can be both known and unfathomable, the answer is that His presence is both inescapable and eternal. What a man brings into this presence is simply himself. For all of us that means: one who is neither completely inaccessible to the truth nor completely open to it.

From such a standpoint it is God who is supremely important. Our ideas, our doctrines, our lives are important only in so far as they point to Him and participate in what He is. And because they always incorporate our limitations, we must always be ready to alter them whenever they prevent us from entering more deeply into what He offers. In other words, our certainty of God goes hand in hand with a *lack* of certainty about the finality of our own formulas. Genuine faith continually breaks the bonds of any concepts, any symbols, any words which try to hold it captive.

Thus the Christian message is, indeed, at a disadvantage wherever men want simple, dogmatic assurance that *their* answers are the right answers. And, more precisely, this is a perennial disadvantage which Protestantism should expect to suffer in comparison with Roman Catholicism. But one does not really succeed in disposing of mystery by demanding something he can control. Nor does one capture mystery by organizing an institution to be its custodian. It surrounds our lives unpredictably at every point. Who understands his own compulsions and his own failure to do what he knows is right? Who understands his ability to enter deeply into communion with some people and his inability to find any common ground with others? Who understands why every assertive step that we take toward bolstering security leads to a fateful increase of insecurity? Who understands why man should have appeared on the scene at all? Who understands the birth of any person or the death of any person?

It is in the midst of such uncertainty about ourselves, and our own righteousness, and our own destiny, that we point beyond ourselves to the Other, as to the constancy of truth itself. Some people reject Christianity because they think it requires pretending to be sure where one is not sure. They look upon the Church as filled with men who claim that their beliefs are absolutely right while everybody else's are wrong. They reject Christianity because the information that we furnish about God does not seem very convincing. And all I can say is that we as ministers and laymen have done a rotten job. Otherwise such people would realize that honesty, humility, and a large dose of skepticism toward neat theories do not exclude a person from faith. On the contrary, they are prerequisites for reaching faith.

This is not quite the last word on the matter, how-

ever, for Christian faith rests upon the singular claim
of one historical life. Surely at this point, one might
think, there can be no tentativeness about our doctrines, our creeds, our formulas. And yet, if what is
true of God is true of Christ, then our certainty attaches to Him, not to ourselves. The same human falli-
bility, the same distortions, the same blindness affect
our interpretations of what Christ means, precisely in
so far as they interfere with our fellowship with God.
Sometimes we overlook this fact. We talk as though
the ultimate nature of God were concealed from us,
while the historicity of Christ makes certain truths as
plain as this morning's headlines. But what we ought
to say is that God is supremely accessible to us in Christ
and supremely mysterious to us in Christ.

Let us be thankful for the accessibility. The message
can be told as a story about events upon this earth. It
breaks through the barriers of sin, reaching the wise
man and the simple man right where they are. For
those who want something tangible and definite, here
it is. But in the next breath we must say that it is unfathomable. What can possibly be less obvious, less
to-be-taken-for-granted, than that God was made man
and took upon Himself the burden of our guilt? Here,
as nowhere else in history, a human life, concrete facts
and events, are linked to inexhaustible meaning.
Christ is, for us, both the mystery and the knowledge
of God.

And it is as though the Epistle to the Colossians were
echoing the eleventh chapter of Romans when it speaks

of "all the riches of assured understanding and the knowledge of God's mystery, of Christ, in whom are hid all the treasures of wisdom and knowledge." (Colossians 2:2–3)

Almighty God, we worship Thee as our Creator and Father, our Redeemer and Judge. Though by searching we cannot find Thee out unto perfection, yet we bless Thee that we know enough of Thy grace to fill our hearts with the strength and peace of trust; enough to comfort and sustain us when life is hard, its crosses heavy and its griefs bitter. We bless Thee as the Father of our Lord Jesus Christ, through whose assurance we find meaning and purpose for our own lives, and in whose name we offer up this prayer to thee. Amen.

GRASPING AND LETTING GO

> Therefore I tell you, do not be anxious about your life, what you shall eat or what you shall drink, nor about your body, what you shall put on. Is not life more than food, and the body more than clothing? . . . Consider the lilies of the field, how they grow; they neither toil nor spin; yet I tell you, even Solomon in all his glory was not arrayed like one of these. But if God so clothes the grass of the field, which today is alive and tomorrow is thrown into the oven, will he not much more clothe you, O men of little faith? . . . But seek first his kingdom and his righteousness, and all these things shall be yours as well.
>
> MATTHEW 6:25, 28–9, 33

YOU AND I HAVE HEARD various interpretations of what it means to seek first the Kingdom of God; but this passage so clearly sets religious trust over against worldly concerns, that most disagreements turn upon the question of whether we can really do this.

Some feel that it *is* possible for men to become so free from anxiety and selfishness that, by means of this inner transformation, economic and political problems will more or less take care of themselves. And they believe that their point of view is the one most faithful to Jesus' real meaning.

Others feel that such an interpretation reduces the

Gospel to sentimental folly. They find in the passage a picture of life in the Kingdom, the chief value of which is to make us aware of how far short we fall. They do *not* believe that we can get rid of anxiety and selfishness completely, but they do find in the Christian message the only adequate diagnosis of our human ills.

Finally there are those who take the passage as a conclusive proof of the fact that Christian ideals are entirely impractical. These people admit quite unashamedly that they take a great deal of thought about what they shall eat and drink and put on. And sometimes they sarcastically suggest that Christians ought to be honest enough to admit that they behave in the same fashion, instead of trying to throw some sort of pious cloak over their desires for economic security and personal success.

Without flattering myself that I can clear up such disputes in a few lines, I should like to call attention to a perfectly familiar and yet rather strange combination of ideas in these words of Jesus. In the process of leading up to His injunction about seeking first the Kingdom of God, He uses an illustration: "Consider the lilies." He draws a contrast between something strained and something effortless. He has been picturing the way men stake their lives on things that *they* can devise by forcing events into patterns of their own making; and He sets this over against what happens when men base their lives on the way God works. In the latter case they receive a kind of security where all lesser concerns fall quietly into perspective.

Therefore, in so far as we enter into a debate over what man can or cannot do in conquering his own selfishness and giving priority to God, the whole argument is beside the point. If the kind of power which Jesus bids us to "seek first" is as effortless as the growth of a flower and as spontaneous as unconditional love, then it reverses all of our usual methods of "seeking." It is as though He were saying: "Human effort can flow *from* God; but when it is cut off from Him, men make a sorry, anxious, self-centered mess of life."

And is it not true that everyone of us knows what this means? No one can live without experiencing at some time or another the surprising and beneficient working of power beyond himself. Maybe it was an impulse of generosity that took him unawares, maybe it was a twinge of conscience that broke through his defenses, maybe it was a sudden alertness to beauty that gripped an otherwise dull and insensitive mind.

This is what a window cleaner on the Empire State building said recently: "You'd think they would keep this place open all night, it's so beautiful at times. I remember a sunrise one time, and it was so beautiful, every nice color in the world, that nobody would believe you if you was to be telling them about it. It's fine up here when you get a gold-and-red-sunrise coming up in back of all those bridges to Brooklyn and Queens. Once I was on the hundred and second floor and it was raining down below. I looked down at the clouds and the lightning, and there I was in the bright sunlight. I felt like God or something."

Many of our contemporaries would scoff at calling such happenings "the work of God"; but even they are glad to accept those precious things of life that come as sheer gifts. Use any words you like — the fact remains that the instant we let go, the instant we stop trying to shove reality, life is enriched instead of being impoverished. Conversely, there is no one alive who is a stranger to the kind of insecurity Jesus is talking about. No one is immune to worry and exhaustion, especially when the things he works for are blocked or ruined.

We are all familiar, then, with the difference between strain and spontaneity; the difference between self-enslavement and freedom; the difference between our way of "working" and God's way of "working." Notice how common assumptions reflect this fact. We can set ourselves to produce beautiful art or music; but if we have no "gift," the result is artificial, no matter how expert it may be technically. We can set ourselves to acquire knowledge and scholarship, but if we lack "insight," the result will be an endless assortment of facts and an empty collection of theories. We can set ourselves to manage human relationships efficiently, but if we lack the kind of sympathy that no amount of striving can acquire, then these relationships will lack depth and substance, no matter how smoothly they may run on the surface.

Therefore we need to ask ourselves most earnestly, whether our lives — not our words, our *lives* — preach this aspect of the Gospel. How much of our planning, our working, our hoping, merely reflects the frenzied pressure and externalism which we criticize so freely in our society? How much of our thinking is a *striving* to reach faith, instead of a dropping of those self-fabricated theories that *prevent* us from reaching it? How much of our worship is a striving to *make* ourselves devout, instead of a glad acceptance of God's gift of Himself?

Almighty God our Father, in those moments when we seem to have reached the end of our own strength, teach us to commit our lives and all that we hold dear to Thy keeping, in the knowledge that Thy wisdom is more certain than all human plans, and Thy mercy is deeper than all human reckoning. Amen.

HOPE

> We triumph even in our troubles, knowing that
> trouble produces endurance, endurance produces char-
> acter, and character produces hope — a hope which
> never disappoints us, since God's love floods our hearts
> through the holy Spirit which has been given to us.

> ROMANS 5:3-5 (Moffatt's translation)

NOTICE THAT THIS SEQUENCE, which ends with hope,
begins with trouble. Yet today many people feel that
the only way they can keep up their hopes is to believe that trouble will not come — or at least that it
will not befall them. To be sure, as events make it increasingly difficult to swallow glowing predictions
about the future, many of our contemporaries have
shifted the argument a bit. One now hears scientists,
political orators, and even some preachers recommend
what they call "the long view." They remind us that
man has only recently appeared upon the planet, that
he is just beginning to learn how to control nature and
himself; and they promise that if we can rise far enough
above the present scene of bloodshed, hatred, and peril
we shall see that everything is going to turn out all
right after all.

This sermon was originally published in *Drew Gateway,*
Spring–Summer, 1953, Drew University, Madison, New Jersey.
Reprinted by permission.

But even this new twist refuses to face tribulation squarely. Instead, it urges us to get away from daily events as far as possible. Thus it tacitly admits that optimism is really useless to the man who must come to grips immediately with persecution, bondage, or death. At its worst, it leaves us well-fed Americans saying to the rest of the world, "We have been let in on the secret of world progress. Provided we are allowed to retain our prosperity, power, and comfort, we can fix everything up. Look at our technology; look at our economic efficiency. If the rest of the world will co-operate instead of throwing obstacles in our path, we can do the job." And we are hurt when Europeans and Asiatics fail to share our kind of confidence.

In so far as this mentality still prevails, it shows how much we need to take to heart St. Paul's words. Undoubtedly he had in mind here the kind of physical hardships and imprisonments that he himself underwent. Indeed, it is sobering to realize how much of the Bible was written by men who were cut off from health, from loved ones, from homeland, and from freedom. But all such instances of trouble fall into perspective when they are seen by men who know the meaning of being cut off from God — and restored to God. Sometimes it is only in the midst of misfortune that we realize fully the value of what we have lost. It is when we are sick that we realize what it means to be healthy; it is *after* a loved one has been stricken that we realize quite how much we love him; it is when we have no zest for work that we realize how joyful creative work can be; it is after a nation has lost its freedom that it realizes how priceless freedom is. So, too, we can understand the longing and restlessness of man only as an awareness, outside the closed gates of Paradise, of the value of a fellowship with God which he has lost. St. Paul begins with tribulation because it is man's lot. It is true of man as man that he must live by hope, if he is to live at all. And the superficiality of optimism can finally be traced back to a forgetfulness of our origin. Instead of trying to bolster confidence by pretending that we human beings can make the future secure, what we really need is that creative power which has set us in the world.

Yet some may feel that we have not given a complete account. It is true that Christian faith stands in sharp contrast with both optimism and despair. But are there not other ways of avoiding these pitfalls? Is it not the case that some of the finest people we know are able to face tribulation, even though they do not embrace Christianity? Undoubtedly we must admit this; and perhaps a sort of Stoic courage is the only viable alternative to Christianity for a thoughtful person today. St. Paul makes a place for courage within his sequence when he speaks of endurance. What he has in mind here is a manly fortitude and constancy in holding out under the trials of life. But it is important to recognize the difference between courage inside and courage outside the framework of Christian faith. In both cases it is admirable. But when courage falls outside belief in God the only form it can take involves a certain withdrawal into the self. The Stoic must simply resolve to maintain his own integrity no matter what the day may bring. Because he has no hope that the tragedies of life can be transmuted by a redemption which comes from beyond himself, he must regard "sticking it out" as an end in itself. On the other hand, Christian endurance is never *mere* endurance. It is able to remain patient, without hurry and without panic because it believes in a God who works redemptively not only in the midst of our trials but also *beyond* them. From this standpoint, the Christian has a firmer confidence in man than anyone else has. He is able to believe that men can learn, can change, can enter into understanding because he is, so to speak, *forbidden* to regard the human race as hopelessly incurable.

It is against such a background that we must seek to understand St. Paul's next word: "character" — or what might be called "tested experience." Perhaps the best way to grasp his meaning is to think, by way of contrast, of what we call the *hardened* character. One of the major problems involved in growing older is that it becomes so easy to assume that we have now learned what to expect of life. So many illusions have been shattered, so many doors have been closed, so much experience has flowed under the bridge, that we are finally compelled to face the facts. Above all, we are compelled to swallow the distasteful knowledge that the facts are not going to change in any radical or miraculous way. For example, when I was a boy I was taught that there could never be another war, that human slavery was a thing of the past, that mankind was becoming increasingly enlightened and kindly, and that as long as Mr. Hoover was alive there was nothing to worry about. I also thought that one could obtain answers to the great philosophical and religious questions merely by studying hard and by becoming more mature.

Undeniably there is always the danger that cumulative experience will lead to world-weariness and hardening, and if we persist in setting our hopes upon particular guarantees and demands, this is almost inevitably the outcome. *There are no finite hopes that are not shatterable;* and if this is the end of the story, then to become mature and to become hopeless are the same thing. Yet St. Paul speaks of a type of character which has learned that everything is not lost because of failure to gain some particular end. He speaks of the sort of man who — perhaps in the very depths of despair — has found fellowship with a power stronger than his despair. No doubt it is dangerous to cite physical illness as an example at this point. Yet I have been told by persons who have entered deeply into suffering that one ordinarily begins by feeling that life will be completely shattered if one does not get well. At this point physical recovery is made virtually equivalent with salvation. But in the end the person cannot meet his illness triumphantly and with inner relaxation until he has learned to define salvation in God's terms instead of his own. Sometimes this represents the turning point which actually leads to physical recovery. But even when complete recovery is impossible, the difference between a serene and a defeated invalid depends upon the same factor.

The truth we are now trying to grasp is always difficult to fathom. I can hardly blame anyone for feeling that religious trust seems like a cultivated indifference toward temporal goods, yet if it really meant that, we would have to renounce it. Surely in the presence of tyranny it is wrong to relinquish one's own rights, the welfare of loved ones, the security of our nation. Surely we must fix our hopes upon promoting *earthly* justice and peace; surely the presence of a sort of dogged resolution may be an indispensable factor in making the realization of these hopes more likely. Why say, then, that the Christian must be ready to relinquish any specific claims? Why say that he must be ready to accept life from God no matter what may happen?

The answer, of course, is that everybody works for finite, temporal goals, but the presence of faith makes a crucial difference as to *how* one works for them. Picture the sort of person who feels that he should be able to control life. He counts on certain things, he insists on his rights, he approaches existence with the attitude that he must demand and seize whatever he is likely to obtain.

The first thing that impresses me about such men is that although they may be able to take calculated risks,

they cannot be venturesome in a really creative way.
Unlike the discoverer, the artist, and the man of faith,
they never set forth not knowing where they are coming out. Therefore they never lay themselves open to
hitherto unimagined perspectives. They cannot tap
any new sources of power. They cannot witness, by
their lives, to the reality of a divine creativity at work
in the world. They live by rigid axioms and by absolute pronouncements, because if life is to be controlled, it must be closed and fixed.

The other thing that impresses me about such men
is that they are almost always bitter. They feel that
somehow life has cheated them. They have tried to
get enough power so that nobody can take advantage
of them; yet the more power they obtain, the more vulnerable they are. Above all, they are terribly solitary
because they have shut themselves up in a fortress of
possessions, attainments, and claims where the releas-
ing breath of the Spirit cannot enter.

In contrast, the man of faith knows — even as he
works for human betterment — that any of his claims
may be taken from him. He knows that ruin can come
— illness, imprisonment, the devastion of his country,
bereavement, death — but he also knows that even in
the midst of such ruin God does not withdraw Himself
from us. This sometimes means that he can find ways
of working, in prison camps, amidst bombed cities,
and against all odds, where others give up. It sometimes means that because of his hope in God he also

is able to retain *earthly* hopes, where others have none of any kind.

But the main point, the surprising point, is that the Christian attitude is actually more realistic. For it is an inescapable fact that the most precious things in life cannot be reached by seizing and demanding at all. Think of the love of a wife or a child. Think of the enjoyment of beauty. Think of friendship. Think of the discovery of truth. Think of the forgiveness of God. The instant we *demand* these things, they disappear. And I can see no hope for us until we learn once again to put things that cannot be obtained by seizure at the top of our scale of values. What we really need for a restoration of *morale* is not some shot in the arm that will keep us working efficiently. What we really need is the assurance that, despite the perils which surround us, and despite the mystery of death which stands at the end of the road, we belong to a fellowship within which we can find abundant life.

This is the only sort of hope which never disappoints us. It is the presence of God's love flooding our hearts as a gift. If it is a gift, does that mean that there is nothing we can do about it? Must we say that some people receive it as a matter of good luck, while others miss it through bad luck? Ask yourself how much it depends on you when you fall in love, or when you possess a given talent. Certainly it is false to say that these things are produced by effort. Try falling in love or acquiring artistic talent by effort some time. But it is equally false to say that what we do makes no difference. A man can turn away from love in order to find a wealthy wife. A man can fritter away his abilities instead of bringing them to fruition. Similarly Christian hope comes to us as a gift, but we can turn away from it and we can fritter it away. To accept the gift is to remain faithful through hours of darkness. To accept the gift is to place all our earthly tribulations and triumphs in God's keeping.

Does trust in Him mean, then, that we are no longer affected by earthly disappointments? Does it mean that we have retired to some mystical haven where nothing temporal can faze us? Obviously not. What it does mean is that, after all false expectations have been abandoned, we still cannot give up on the human race because God has not given up on us. It means that, although we attach full weight to every tragedy and evil, we find no combination so ruinous that the only honest thing is to abandon our trust in God. Let us put this to a test. Let us make a list, in imagination, of one thing after another which might be taken from us. At what point would we be compelled to say that human existence is a gruesome accident instead of a gift from God? The New Testament is far ahead of us, for it is already standing at the extreme end of the list where man confronts death. At this point everything is taken away from us. And it is precisely in the face of death that the Christian faith has always known that to abandon hope is to abandon love.

The real core of our belief in eternal life is not the anticipation of some condition that we can specify and imagine. At this point Christians have always needed to be on their guard against illusions — even selfish, egocentric illusions. Our hope is one that never disappoints because it cannot be undermined by time at all. The presence of God, of which the Apostle speaks, is the presence of an eternal love. It is only on *this* basis that we enter into a fellowship that is not destroyed by death. Surely, then, if we ever cease to hope for mankind, if we ever cease to believe that communion with God is man's destiny, in that same instant we have ceased to love.

The sequence with which we began ends by pointing our gaze beyond time. Yet every step in the sequence is rooted in present experience — trouble, endurance, character, hope. Each of these steps is seen in the light of what God has *already* done for us in Christ. What we believe about life and what we believe about the end of life are the same thing. Creation and Resurrection come from one and the same God. And therefore the "new life" in Christ is always both a return and a transfiguration. It is restoration of a fellowship which God has *always* offered; yet it is also entrance into a "new" fellowship where we really find ourselves, and other men, and God, as though for the first time.

Almighty Father, we humbly acknowledge Thy large and tender providence toward us; our manifold and abundant sources of refreshment and security; the hidden mercies of Thy Spirit; and the gracious results of life's discipline. We thank Thee for the presence of those we love; and for all the things which, amid care and strife, enrich and gladden our lives. Above all, we thank Thee for the coming of Thy Son Jesus Christ into this world of sin and sorrow, through whose gift of Himself we may seek Thy forgiveness and hope for life eternal. Amen.

WHAT BINDS MEN TOGETHER

And as he entered a village, he was met by ten lepers, who stood at a distance and lifted up their voices and said, "Jesus, Master, have mercy on us." When he saw them he said to them, "Go and show yourselves to the priests." And as they went they were cleansed. Then one of them, when he saw that he was healed, turned back, praising God with a loud voice; and he fell on his face at Jesus' feet, giving him thanks. Now he was a Samaritan. Then said Jesus, "Were not ten cleansed? Where are the nine? Was no one found to return and give praise to God except this foreigner?" And he said to him, "Rise and go your way; your faith has made you well."

LUKE 17:12–19

WE CANNOT HELP but be disturbed by the fact that our Christian faith so often seems irrelevant when we are called upon to make momentous practical decisions. We get the feeling that we are living in a secularized country and a secularized world. We see the patterns of the future looming before us, and in our candid moments we admit that these patterns will be formed largely as a result of political, economic, and military considerations. When religion comes into the picture at all, it comes in as a sort of holy frosting upon a very earthy cake.

And we realize that something is wrong. We know

86

that our most precious ideals have come down to us
from the Christian traditions. We know that if the
patterns of the future are shaped without regard to a
Christian view of the individual and a Christian view
of society, our prospects are dark indeed. In short, we
know that unless we can unite in bringing about a
spiritually restored humanity, we relinquish the future to those who will fashion it in terms of organized
tyranny.

It is against such a background that I wish to suggest three fundamental principles which Christianity
offers as a basis for national life.

The first is this: Although security and order must
be maintained, the highest function of the state is to
promote a co-operative fellowship. Often we get so
preoccupied with the coercive functions of government that we lose sight of its spiritual responsibilities
entirely.

Let me illustrate what I mean. In the story of the
ten lepers, one fact arrests our attention immediately.
It took leprosy to bridge the gap between the Jews and
Samaritans. Had it not been for their common misfortune, these men would have had no dealings with
each other. We are reminded of that other story where
Jesus tells of a Samaritan whose kindness put the
Priest and the Levite to shame. For the irony is apparent when He asks, "Is this stranger the only one
who returns to give glory to God?" It is as though He
were saying something like this: "Here is a man whom

you would not accept as a companion until a terrible disease made all of you outcasts. Then for a while you forgot your racial hatreds, and one might have supposed that you had learned something about how to live together. But apparently this Samaritan is the only one who has learned anything for he alone has returned to give glory to God."

In this situation we have vivid proof of the old saying that misery loves company. But a terrible fact underlies the saying. Sometimes we cannot love company until we have first become miserable ourselves. There are ties which bind men together, but often we do not discover them except in the midst of common misfortune.

These ties even reach beyond human relations; for they seem to form the fabric of all life. I once heard an explorer tell how his party was trapped by a forest fire and finally found refuge on an island in the middle of a river. The island was crowded with animals of every kind, which had also been driven there; and the men were forced to spend the night surrounded by beasts of prey. Yet throughout their vigil, as the fire raged on the opposite bank of the river, no living thing harmed another. Men and beasts had forgotten their enmities in the face of a common peril.

A similar principle seems to underlie the origin and growth of human government. In the presence of natural dangers, men learn how to band together for food, clothing, and shelter. In the presence of a powerful foe, people learn how to unite for mutual defense.

A naval officer has told me of the sense of solidarity which he felt on his battleship. He would be certain that in a moment of peril any man on the ship would be ready to lay down his life, if need be, for the sake of the others. One day, while he was riding on a New York subway, this officer got to wondering what would happen if an accident occurred there. He knew that there would probably be a mad scramble for the nearest exit. Now what made the difference? If you asked a sailor why he would willingly risk his life for the others, he might say: "Because we're all Americans." But all the people on the subway were Americans, too. So this officer finally decided that it was the fact of common danger, confronted repeatedly, that had welded the men on his ship into a unit, where each individual reacted automatically, without a moment's hesitation, for the welfare and protection of the whole group.

Indeed, one could go on indefinitely reading the pages of history, and writing at the top of almost every page: "It took peril and misery to bring men together."

Even in the most intimate personal relationships we often do not recognize our human kinship until something stabs us into wakefulness. Mathew Arnold writes:

Ah, love, let us be true
To one another! for the world, which seems
To lie before us like a land of dreams,
So various, so beautiful, so new,

Hath really neither joy, nor love, nor light,
Nor certitude, nor peace, nor help for pain;
And we are here as on a darkling plain
Swept with confused alarms of struggle and flight,
Where ignorant armies clash by night.

(Dover Beach)

We all know of homes which have themselves been like darkling plains "swept with confused alarms of struggle and flight, where ignorant armies clash by night." We know of homes where there has been discord, where the members of the family have gone on from day to day, heedless of how much they mean to each other, until some tragedy has suddenly knit them together. Yes, even of family affection we must say that sometimes it takes misery to make clear the ties which have been there all along.

Now what all this comes down to is that men are created for fellowship, and sometimes we rediscover this fact only through the suffering and disaster which result when we fail to fulfill the conditions of fellowship. This is the sword of Damocles over our heads, which makes our human institutions necessary. Benjamin Franklin once said of the colonies: "We must indeed all hang together, or, most assuredly, we shall all hang separately." And his words apply today, not merely to this country, but to every nation, to every race, and to every class. They might be rendered in a modern version: "We must indeed all harmonize together, or most assuredly we shall all be atomized separately."

Now we can accept this harsh condition as a blessing only as we learn from it. After all, what do we think of a nation which can be united only for purposes of self-defense and never for purposes of social reconstruction? What do we think of allies who work together only so long as circumstances force them to? What do we think of a family which holds a reunion only when there is a funeral to be conducted and a will to be read?

Self-interest and self-protection force men to band together. But this is merely the negative basis for fellowship and it will not suffice in the moment when men need some constructive meaning which they freely unite in promoting.

That leads directly to our second principle: Christianity alone can bring us back to a realization of the true ends of life.

The whole trouble with a fellowship founded solely upon self-interest is that it has no real permanence or substance. The story of the lepers reminds us of this fact when it tells that nine of the men quickly became heedless of the source of their recovery. Think for a moment of how much human behavior they typify. They cry out in despair for a boon from the Master; but as soon as they are healed, they take the gifts of fortune for granted. They have not really learned anything through their suffering.

Are not most of us like them? After World War II, how long did it take us to forget the principles on

which an enduring peace can be based? How long did
it take the old destructive animosities between ourselves and other nations, or between groups within
this nation, to break out afresh? How much did we
really learn through our suffering?

The answer to that question depends upon whether
the religious seriousness which the war fostered and
which a precarious world situation can sometimes
help keep alive turns out to be something deeply-
rooted, or merely a passing phase. It depends upon
whether we have learned that the great ethical principles which undergird freedom and justice must be
fulfilled at all times, and not merely when it suits our
convenience.

The trouble with the nine lepers was that they used
their encounter with Christ merely as a means to
their own ends, and then forgot Him. But what He
stands for cannot be forgotten with impunity. I believe it is wrong to assume that the so-called "plain
man" does not care about God, salvation, and eternal
life. To be sure, he does not care about high-flown
theories; but he does care about the worth of his
own life, and the lives of his fellows, beyond eating,
sleeping, working, procreating, and dying. However
inarticulately, he wants something better than blind
fate governing his affairs. He does not want to be like
the White Knight in *Alice in Wonderland* who
mounted his horse backwards and was carried away
rapidly in one direction while he was facing all the
time in the opposite direction. He wants to turn

around and take hold of the reins. He does not want
to be a victim of mass social forces which sweep mankind headlong from one war to another. He wants to
stand upon his feet as a child of God to build a new
society in co-operation with the will of God. And if
this is true, it means that our age needs the Christian
faith — a faith that calls man to his high destiny as a
spiritual being instead of as a cog in a vast machine.

Therefore our third principle is this: The creation
of a new society must begin with the creation of a
new individual. God redeems men into a community
— but He redeems them one by one.

I like to think of the Samaritan in our story as a
symbol of this message. His significance is due to the
fact that he has been lifted out of this pattern where
fellowship lasts only so long as circumstances demand
it, and is forgotten as soon as the peril has passed. By
responding to the power of Christ, he has entered into
a new relationship with God and with his fellow
men.

Every new departure in human history has to begin with an individual. Every great reform, every
great institution, begins with some lone figure who
says: "Here I stand, I can do no other." But we have
fallen into the habit of regarding ourselves as pup-
pets; we feel so completely at the mercy of economic
and political forces, that we think of ourselves as
flotsam tossed about by the waves of the future.
Therefore we look to the state, or to some plan for a

new world order, for our salvation. But under such circumstances it is not surprising if we frequently fall into cynicism or despair.

The state can do nothing, and there can be no new world order, except as the hearts and minds of individuals are transformed. This is the message which the Christian Gospel has proclaimed from the beginning, and we can ill afford to forget it today.

And if you ask about the secret of this transformation, my answer is that only through Christian faith can a man come into touch with the forgiving power of God. By forgiveness I do not mean the abrogation of justice. I mean employing the instruments of justice *without* vindictiveness and *with* a penitent realization of our own share of guilty responsibility for the tragedies of these times.

Oscar Levant tells a story about several gifted children who were playing before Paderewski. One little girl played nicely until a final arpeggio, where she missed her aim and the effect made the piano sound as though it had been wired with bed springs. She began to cry. Then Paderewski came over and kissed her on the forehead — which is something she would not have gotten if she had played it right.

Of course the whole point of the story turns upon the fact that Paderewski was not indifferent to music. That is why his forgiveness meant something.

Well, at an infinitely higher level, there is another story which men have been hearing for centuries now. It is a story about One who was born in a manger and

who died upon a Cross. And the whole point of that
story turns upon the fact that God is not indifferent
about human misery and sin. That is why His forgiveness means something.

There are possibilities for binding up the wounds
of our suffering world, there are possibilities for
finding a lasting basis for fellowship, if we really
learn through the agony of these past years. The great
instruments of government, and the vast machinery
of our civilization, can be used to build a society
which will bring blessedness instead of slavery to
men. But this can happen only as we are bound together by the ties of a common gratitude and a common salvation, as we stand — one by one — like that
Samaritan, in the presence of Christ.

*O God, by whose power we are created and by
whose love we are redeemed, hearken, we beseech
Thee, unto the prayers of a desperate and sinful
world. Restore us from sickness to newness of life,
chasten the oppressor and rescue the oppressed, re-
place our enmities with penitence and our anxieties
with trust. Above all, draw us by Thy Spirit into the
unity of that faith wherein we are made mindful of
Thy mercy, through Jesus Christ our Lord. Amen.*

THE LOVE OF GOD AND SUFFERING

Now his elder son was in the field; and as he came and drew near to the house, he heard music and dancing. And he called one of the servants and asked what this meant. And he said to him, 'Your brother has come, and your father has killed the fatted calf, because he has received him safe and sound.' But he was angry and refused to go in. His father came out and entreated him, but he answered his father, 'Lo, these many years I have served you, and I never disobeyed your command; yet you never gave me a kid, that I might make merry with my friends. But when this son of yours came, who has devoured your living with harlots, you killed for him the fatted calf!' And he said to him, 'Son, you are always with me, and all that is mine is yours. It was fitting to make merry and be glad, for this your brother was dead, and is alive; he was lost, and is found.'

LUKE 15:25–32

THE OTHER DAY I was reading a chapter on the problem of evil by a famous philosopher. In it he painted a familiar picture of the agonies, bafflements, and injustices of life. Then he concluded, as though no one had ever thought of this conclusion before, that it is obviously impossible to believe in God. Although this philosopher has probably been subject to his share of unfair treatment, pain, and bereavement, he also happens to be a man who has spent his whole life in the safety of an academic environment, enjoying good health, a good income, and a good reputation.

Therefore I could not help but put his words alongside some others I had read recently wherein a minister recounts the following incident: "Many years ago as a young man I was preaching on the love of God; there was in the congregation an old Polish Jew who had been converted to the Christian faith. He came to me afterward and said: 'You have no right to speak of the love of God, until you have seen, as I have seen, a massacre of Jews in Poland — until you have seen, as I have seen, the blood of your dearest friends running in the gutters on a grey winter morning.' I asked him later how it was that, having seen such a massacre, *he* had come to believe in the love of God. The answer he gave in effect was that the Christian gospel first began to lay hold of him because it bade him see God — the love of God — as it were just where he was, just where he could not but always be in his thought and memories — in those blood-stained streets on that grey morning. It bade him see the love of God — not somewhere else, but in the midst of just that sort of thing, in the blood and agony of Calvary. He did at least know, he said, that this was a message that grappled with the facts; and then he went on to say something the sense of which I shall always remember though the words I have forgotten. He said, 'As I looked at that man upon the Cross . . . I knew I was at a point of final crisis and decision in my life; I knew I must make up my mind once and for all, and either take my stand beside Him and share in His undefeated faith in God . . . or else fall finally into a bottomless pit of bitterness, hatred and unutterable despair.' " *

Admittedly we cannot generalize upon the basis of these contrasting passages. We cannot assume that all skeptical philosophers remain skeptical merely because they have not suffered enough; and we cannot assume that one can reach genuine faith only through travail as terrible as that which befell this Polish Jew. But they clearly occupy two different levels; the Jew understands suffering more deeply precisely because he had to struggle so hard to find meaning in it, and what he had to struggle against was a fact — a purge — and not an idea.

Interestingly enough, the philosopher admits that his conclusions lead to pessimism; but anyone who reads his words can see that he keeps his despair polite by means of his urbane intelligence. On the other hand, the Polish Jew can place no intellectual cushions between himself and his despair. In a situation where thinking cannot alter the facts one whit, he is driven into a faith that is commensurate with the depth of his suffering.

Hence we *can* generalize at least to this extent: for the Polish Jew makes us see that our capacity to withstand suffering depends upon something *beyond ourselves* which makes acceptance of it meaningful.

* From *God and Men* by Herbert H. Farmer. Copyright 1947 by Stone & Pierce. By permission of Abingdon Press.

We must place this incident in sharp contrast to the idea that if God is real, then things should go well with decent people and things should go ill with wicked people. Of course, if you were asked point blank whether you entertained such an idea you would deny it; you would say that it belongs to a conception of distributive justice which Christianity has transcended. Nevertheless, deep down among our hopes and fears the ancient conception dies hard. We instinctively feel that if certain tragedies befall ourselves, or our loved ones, or worthy people anywhere, then the universe simply *is not fair*.

Needless to say, Christian faith does not ask us to abandon our concern for justice. But it does show us that anyone who concentrates exclusively upon whether he is getting his "just deserts" in life has not yet entered fully into the meaning of the Gospel. The older brother in the story of the Prodigal Son had what might be called reasonable grounds for complaint; but if he had really loved his brother, his complaints would have been swallowed up in joy at his return. And is it not true, in every aspect of life, that a legalistic frame of mind automatically excludes us from reaching the highest levels of spiritual beatitude? Within friendship, a contractual agreement can be a sensible and convenient tool; but without friendship, no amount of insistence upon a contract can force a man to be fair and generous in his motives. Within the love of marriage, a legal arrangement can protect the blessings of monogamy; but without love in the relationship, what would be more ridiculous than to say that the marriage certificate has legally obligated one's mate to be patient and affectionate? And at the theological level surely we are confronted with a clear decision. We can insist that the universe should bestow good fortune upon men in a manner correlative with their virtue. Or we can believe that God's purpose is supremely disclosed in the sufferings of a sinless man. But it is quite impossible to combine the two convictions.

As one writer has put it: "No man who is aware of God's presence can regard himself as in a strong position for making demands. He will realize that, once strictness gets started, God can always, so to speak, overbid him. If we shout: 'I demand justice!' a voice from Heaven will reply, like an echo, 'I demand justice.' Who is bold enough to think that he can pass this test? But if we fall on our knees and cry out: 'Grace!' the answer comes back from Heaven: 'Grace.' " *

And yet, lest we seem to be forgetting the agony of countless human beings whose fate really *does* outrage our sense of justice, lest we seem to be forgetting those moments when we pray for relief and mercy, not for ourselves, but for *others,* let us remember that

* This passage is a running paraphrase of the concluding pages of Kierkegaard's *Works of Love.* The full selection can be found in *Works of Love* (Princeton University Press), 1946, pp. 308–310.

the light which the Cross sheds upon suffering discloses an invitation, not an explanation. It is an act on God's part, calling for an act on our part. If offers a faith that can be stronger than despair; but it leaves us dismayed by those who have not discerned and reached such faith. Perhaps the worst suffering we are ever called upon to undergo is encountered at that point where we cannot *transfuse* into someone dear to us the resources that might save him. Sometimes the only thing that love can do is to suffer for and with another person who himself finds no meaning at all in his suffering.

Yet it remains true, even in such moments, that the more we love, the more we are brought into the presence of God Himself, who does not force men into faith. We are brought into the presence of Christ, who goes to the Cross in disclosing the meekness, patience, and travail whereby the power of God deals with the agonies of men.

O Thou, who art the Light of Life, we thank Thee for the many riches and blessings which Thou bestowest upon us beyond anything we can earn or achieve. In the quiet of the night when we are asleep, Thy moon and Thy stars shine above us in the heavens. Thou dost not leave us in darkness at any time. Even in our saddest experiences, we are not left without a Comforter. In the valley of the shadow of death Thou art with us — seeking our good all through the times of our ignorance and doubt and fear, of our sorrow and pain and sin. In this faith we pray unto thee, through Jesus Christ our Lord. Amen.

II

He was wounded for our transgressions, he was bruised for our iniquities: the chastisement of our peace was upon him; and with his stripes we are healed.

ISAIAH 53:5 (K.J.V.)

What does the service of Holy Communion tell us about the love of God and suffering? I suggest that regardless of denominational ties, every Christian can find two basic meanings in the service that is the central act of our worship.

In the first place, it means that *we have fellowship with a forgiving instead of a condemming God.* From the beginning of time, men have been tempted to think of God on the model of their own ideas of power and justice. They have pictured Him as governing the world from afar — punishing the guilty and rewarding the virtuous. Now Christianity does not deny, or course, that God is powerful and just; but it declares that His power and justice are expressed through love. This means something so different from the way we try to run our lives that most men still cannot get it through their heads. For it means that God does not simply order men about,

force them to do this or that, smash evil, and guarantee the success of the righteous. Primarily He
achieves His purpose only through a transformation
of man himself, a conversion of the heart. And this
means that He strives to win us out of our selfishness
and sin into a love that can be genuine because it is a
free response of gladness and gratitude.

To be sure God does set limits to human evil. But
when wickedness brings disaster down upon our heads,
it is not sent by a cruel tyrant in Heaven. For the most
part, disaster is a consequence of our own refusal to
respond to Him. Think of the appalling evils of our
time, and you will realize that they spring from men
who are incapable of admitting their own need for forgiveness and are therefore unable to respond when
God offers it to them. Now God knows, better than we
do, that amidst such circumstances, the innocent suffer
with the guilty. He knows that no individual can be
safe until the whole human race has come to its senses.
And he knows that, in the meantime, enmity will repeatedly seem to triumph over love. In immediate situations we have to defend ourselves against ruthless
people, but we all know that there can be no final
solution until the ruthless men's hearts and our hearts
have somehow been changed.

The same thing is true in personal relationships.
Sometimes we have to stop the wickedness of another
individual by means of threats or punishment. But
in the end the only effective way to change the sinner
himself requires that we climb down off the pedestal

of self-righteousness so that we can take our place alongside him. We can stop him, perhaps, by force. But we can win his heart only by identifying ourselves with his own needs, and by suffering with him and for him until he is able to respond to us in trust and love.

The Christian Gospel tells us that God does not stand aloof from us, insisting that we must first become virtuous people before we can come into His presence. Instead, He comes right into the midst of human events, in the person of Jesus Christ, taking upon Himself the burden of our sin, identifying Himself with our sufferings. He comes to serve, not the self-righteous who think that they are all right anyway, but the sinner. And He attaches no conditions to His offer except the repentant acknowledgment on our part that we do need our hearts transformed.

I repeat: from the beginning of time men have fashioned pictures of God's power. But God cuts athwart all our human ideas by an *act*. He comes to mankind as a babe born in a manger. He teaches us the meaning of faith through One who cares nothing for prestige, worldly power, and riches. And by the gift of His Son on the Cross, He makes us realize that to win the human race from sin and bondage is far harder than to move the stars in their courses.

First of all, then, Communion means fellowship with this God of suffering love. And the sacrament means a contrite acceptance of His gift to us as we

receive His forgiveness. Only so can we ever become
acceptable to ourselves. If anyone feels unworthy as
he approaches the Lord's Table, let him remember
that he cannot conceal this unworthiness from God.
But let him also remember that he *need not* conceal
it. The Table is set for sinners. We do not have to
become perfect before we are allowed to come before
it. Rather, we receive here that divine mercy and
nurture which alone can make us better men and
women.

In the second place, *this fellowship with a suffering
God is the answer to the mystery of our human suffering.* We are all familiar with the fact that people
are tempted to lose their faith in God when terrible
events befall them. All of us have heard someone say:
"I can't believe in God any more, because if there is a
God, why does He permit war, why does he allow ac-
cidents to happen, why does He let my loved ones
die?"

Now the Bible does not run away from terrible
facts like these. How could it? How can any of us run
away from them? But one of the most remarkable
things about the Bible is its account of how men have
found their faith raised to the highest level, at precisely that point where one expects them to lose it.

Think of Abraham. In the moment when Isaac lies
ready for sacrifice upon the altar, Abraham's steadfast trust teaches him the deepest meaning of fellowship with God. Once Luther's wife said that she could

not believe the Abraham and Isaac story because God would never expect anyone to treat his son that way. And Luther replied, "But Katie, God *did* treat His Son that way."

Or think of Isaiah. He sees the servant of God as one who is despised and rejected of men, a man of sorrows, and acquainted with grief. He sees that people do not receive exactly what they deserve in this life. He sees that the innocent suffer along with the guilty. But what saves Isaiah from utter despair is the realization that when the innocent suffer *for the sake of* mankind, then God is working redemptively through them. "He was wounded for our transgressions, he was bruised for our iniquities; the chastisement of our peace was upon him; and with his stripes we are healed."

Or think of Job. The long-winded speeches of his friends cannot explain the dreadful things which have happened to him. So in his misery Job is driven away from all human answers. Finally he appeals to God Himself. Only in this situation is he able to say: "Though He slay me, yet will I trust Him." Only in this situation is he able to say: "I know that my Redeemer liveth."

Think, finally, of Jesus Christ Himself. Here at last we understand the pilgrimage of these men in the Old Testament. Here at last we find light for our own pilgrimage. For when we think of that figure upon the Cross, we know that He too had to cling to trust in the face of despair. He still calls out *"My*

God, *my* God" even in the moment when He feels utterly forsaken. And it is only because He can pass through this moment of dereliction that He is able to say, at the end: "Father, into thy hands I commit my spirit."

What all this means is that the Christian answer to suffering is not a theory: it is a fellowship. In reply to our doubts it offers not an idea, but a man — a man in communion with God. And surely this is the only possible answer. When you and I try to comfort someone in grief, we know that words and ideas are peculiarly futile. But that does not matter. For what the grieving person needs most is not our words, but ourselves.

Christianity does not mean that we should run out in search of suffering. The Gospel does not tell us to seek salvation by tormenting ourselves as much as possible. But at the center of Christian faith stands the fact that *in so far as we have learned the meaning of love, suffering is inevitable.* The more you love your child, the more vulnerable you are to suffering when trouble befalls that child. The more you love your neighbor — whether he is on the next street or in Korea — the more you enter into his perils, his pains, his death. Is it any wonder, then, that when the Gospel tries to tell us about God, it simply speaks of father-love and neighbor-love? You and I cannot run away from such suffering either. Therefore, because of Him, you and I never have to face tragedy alone.

Because of Him, we can take the worst that befalls us, and instead of being driven into bitterness, we find here the source of our deepest communion with God. For He is a God who can turn the crime of Calvary into the glory of Easter.

In our hour of need, God sends us, not an idea, but a person, Jesus Christ through whom He bestows upon us Himself and His love. In the same hour, let us answer by giving God not words, but a person, namely, ourselves, our hearts and wills. At the center of the Communion Service is something we *do,* rather than something we say. The bread and the wine are symbols of what God has given to us. Let them also stand for the fact that we, here and now, offer our bodies and souls in response to Him.

Almighty and Most Gracious God, Thou who art the refuge of Thy children in every time of need, hear us, we beseech Thee, as we pray for Thy help — whenever our hearts grow cold and life seems bleak, whenever evil memories trouble us and we mourn over hopes unrealized, whenever we are tempted to shut ourselves off from others, whenever we are called upon to fulfill tasks that seem beyond our strength, whenever the unknown future troubles us and we forget Thine eternal love and care. Grant to us, O God, in all such moments, that confidence in Thy strength and mercy which alone can support us in every danger and carry us through every trial, so that we may offer up our lives to thee, through Jesus Christ our Lord. Amen.

BRINGING AND RECEIVING

And the Word became flesh and dwelt among us.

JOHN 1:14

This cup is the new covenant in my blood. Do this, as often as you drink it, in remembrance of me. For as often as you eat this bread and drink the cup, you proclaim the Lord's death until he comes.

I CORINTHIANS 11:25–6

Holy Father, keep them in Thy name which Thou hast given me, that they may be one, even as we are one.

JOHN 17:11

This is my body which is broken for you.

I CORINTHIANS 11:24

IN THE SACRAMENT of the Lord's Supper the meaning of our faith is drawn together and expressed as in no other way. And it is possible to characterize this meaning without becoming embroiled in controversy or in partisan interpretation. All we need do is to meditate upon the amazing contrast between what we bring to the Table and what we receive from it.

This sermon was originally published in *Pulpit Digest*, March 1953 under the title "On the Meaning of the Lord's Supper." Reprinted by permission.

In the first instance we bring to it bread and wine as symbols of *the natural world,* signifying the fact that we are creatures who must feed our bodies in order to live. Our age has formed the habit of trying to look at nature "by itself," and when viewed by itself the world undeniably loses the marks of sacredness. There are marks of beauty and of frightening power here; but nature, as a whole, confronts us as a vast, impersonal system. We can try to utilize and exploit it; but in the end we face a situation of "man against darkness." The physical universe swallows us in death as heedlessly as it brought us to birth.

But through the transforming presence of Christ at the Communion Table, we realize that we do not have to confront nature "by itself." What are the bread and the wine if taken by themselves? A bundle of chemical compounds. To dissociate them from what they signify at the Lord's Table is to do violence, not only to our own thoughts, but also to the meaning of the material world. For no aspect of that world, no bodily activity, no facet of earthly life can be separated from the creative and redemptive work of God. We know very well that in many respects the world we bring to this Table is *not* sacred. We have only to think of how we use natural resources, atomic power, economic wealth, and our own bodies. But because the Word was made flesh, because Christ came into this world of creatureliness and sin, the final word of our faith about nature is that it is the medium through which the sacred is expressed. This is a sacramental universe. Our mission is not to fly away from the body or from secular tasks. Our mission as Protestants is to let God hallow the physical world, creaturely needs, and the common life, so that though they be as mundane as bread and wine, they shall at the same time be indwelt by His Spirit.

In this we fail continually, even though at this Table we realize that God has not failed us. Now why do we fail? One reason is that our approach to the natural world is so often one of utility. Amidst our efforts to control and exploit, the sacrament of the Lord's Supper brings us up with a halt, for it has no utility at all. What, from a practical standpoint, does it accomplish? Some people come together, partake of tiny portions of bread and wine, and then go home again. How can we afford to waste time doing this, when there are so many pressing problems calling for our attention? One part of the answer is that only those who approach nature in an attitude of communion can grasp its sacred character. What we bring to the Table is a distorted, modern view of the physical universe. What we receive is an eternal truth, all but buried and forgotten in our daily lives.

In the second place we bring to this service *the transitoriness of those daily lives*. No human relationship can be safeguarded against the ravages of change. No attainment, no friendship, no love, can be preserved unaltered even in memory. And at the end, time threatens to take from us not only everything we have cherished, but also our very selves. Yet such thoughts are one-sided because every new life is also borne of time, and every moment is an opening of new doors as well as a closing of old ones. Time is the scene of all creation as well as of all destruction. The real tragedy is not that our lives must pass, but that they pass in such a scattered fashion. Life seems like an idiot's tale to many people because they have found nothing to tie its ends together. They declare that they are working hard so that someday they can enjoy peace and security. But the things worked for will turn out to be disappointing even if attained. Define in your own mind what you mean by an adequate income or adequate recognition. Is there such a thing? Can you find any ceiling for your desires? Is there any point at which you will really be satisfied?

No, if anything can tie time together it is to be found inside, not outside; it is to be found in ourselves. Yet what have we to offer when we bring ourselves to this Table? Are you able to bring your whole past — every moment of it? Can you say: "A single theme of fidelity has given unity to my life through all the movements of the years"? No. When we bring our memories before the Table, we realize that our lives cry out for a transforming presence. And what of the future? Can you say: "Here every plan, every ambition can be disclosed, for they are offered in the service of a meaning which time cannot destroy"?

Our Christian faith declares that history, like nature, is the bearer of the sacred. We are not to seek God by running away from it; we are not to curse

fate because all things pass and death stands at the
end. For we encounter God in history. And therefore what ties time together is encountered in the
present. Yet we have not hallowed our fragmentary
lives nor the ghastly course of human history. What
we bring to this Table is a long, tormenting story of
shattered hopes and future fears; we bring the story
of a race which has failed to find, in the rise and fall
of its empires, a meaning that time cannot destroy.

What, then do we receive? We receive a memory, a
presence, and a future. We do this in remembrance
of Him, for the blessed assurance of His presence, and
to show the Lord's death till He come. Here our
chastening memories, our faltering present decisions,
and our misgivings about the future undergo a transfiguration. Our personal histories and human history
are taken up into the forgiving power of God, who is
Alpha and Omega. By memory we find Him in the
Man of Nazareth; by hope we find Him in the pledge
of His coming again; by faith we find Him here, now.
The transitoriness of our lives is tied together by the
abiding presence of God in Jesus Christ.

Hence it is appropriate that the meaning of the
Lord's Supper is conveyed by an act rather than by
words. Words, ideas, can have a certain timelessness.
Once uttered, if they are true, they are true forever.
But it is only by act that the Eternal can *be* in time.
The abiding character of divine fellowship must be
acted out, for it cannot merely be spoken about. We
commit our whole lives to God through a sacrament

which lies deeper than concepts and theories. And it is especially important to us, as Protestants, thus to *actualize* fellowship, lest we spend all our time in merely speaking or hearing about it from the pulpit.

We also bring to this Table *our isolation*. Loneliness takes many forms; but what I have in mind has nothing to do with what are sometimes called "social contacts." I am thinking rather of the fact that the bonds between people can be so imperfect, so treacherous that a man may go through his whole life without ever having found genuine understanding and acceptance. Because men are created for fellowship, they find isolation intolerable. Yet where is that fellowship which will never betray, never enslave, never become idolatrous? Many of the falsehoods we speak, and the crimes we commit, are not chosen deliberately at all. We find ourselves swept into them because the alternative would mean defying some group to which we belong, risking an ostracism we cannot endure. Many of these group loyalties may be worthy and necessary. Yet think of the terrible things men have done for the sake of family, political party, nation, or church! We sell our souls because of the need to belong to something greater than ourselves. Yet do we ever fully overcome the feeling that other human beings are strange and alien? In our times, solidarity too often means the death of freedom and conscience. But we also know that freedom and conscience cannot flourish if a person has to cut himself off from human ties. We bring to the Lord's

Table ourselves and our world, torn asunder in a struggle between sick isolation and sick collectivism.

And what we receive here is perfect fellowship which releases instead of enslaving the self. What is offered must be accepted voluntarily, otherwise it is not truly received at all. The bond between Christ and His people is a spiritual one — that is, Person to person. There can be no question of enhancing the community at the expense of the individual, or the individual at the expense of the community. Here the barriers which make men strangers to each other disappear — differences of language, color, denomination, and tradition are swallowed up in a single act of participation. Churchmen may make pronouncements about the forms connected with this act; but no pronouncements can fetter the presence of God, available to all mankind. It is nothing less than this which the Eucharist offers.

Therefore we bring to it all the imperfections of our earthly societies: the misunderstandings of family life, the partisan character of our political loyalties, the tyrannies that we suffer and impose through social relations. We are not bidden to run away from these ties as monks who have nothing to do with marriage, politics, and secular struggles. But we are bidden to find here, and here alone, that fellowship which can transmute all lesser loyalties, and at the same time put an end to our isolation.

Finally, we bring *our suffering* to this Table. Let us not utter one sentimental word in an effort to gloss over its poignancy. This *is* the point, above all, where life seems meaningless and intolerable. Think of your own worst moments, realize how little they showed on the surface, and then recall how many people you meet may be masking something equally tormenting. If you harbor any easy answers to the problem of suffering, they become empty when you think of the travail of your own dearest friend.

We are not bidden to run away from sufferings; and what good would it do if we were? We bring them to the Lord's Table because, in the end, that is all we can do with them.

Recall that the things we have already mentioned are not sacred *before* we carry them into God's presence. Nature by itself is not sacred; and neither is human history. Likewise, our sufferings taken by themselves are not sacred. What is holy about cancer, insanity, poverty, and persecution? Suffering, taken by itself, is evil, and our Lord devoted His life to the battle against it.

Yet it is in *His* suffering, it is in the offering of His own body and blood, that our suffering may be made sacred. As in all fellowship, here in the Lord's Supper, the giving and receiving move both ways. By receiving this bread and wine we take into our lives the nurture and healing of God. And by forgiveness He takes our sufferings upon Himself so that He is present in the very midst of them.

Notice that the Christian faith, at all these points, is never a running away. It is a coming forward. We bring an offering and we receive an offering. We bring a broken world, a broken humanity, broken selves. In return we receive broken bread. And by the transforming presence of Christ, that which was broken is made whole again. What we receive is a sacramental universe, time tied together, true community, and redemption.

Surely if this sacrament is accepted with fidelity, such a service inevitably issues in action. What is central here is an act of God in which we can participate only through deeds, not words. Yet because some of us are forever seeking to solve human problems *merely* by doing something, it is important to acknowledge the sense in which in the administration of the elements we human beings do very little. The only thing we can accomplish is a presentation, a coming forward, of ourselves, in order that something may be done in us. Unless God is redemptively present in all of nature, in all time, in all human societies, in all suffering, this service cannot make Him present. It is He, through Christ, who has consecrated all of life. Therefore we consecrate these elements.

Eternal God our Father, grant that in communion with Thee the way that lieth before us shrouded in uncertainty and darkness may become clear. If we have come in grief, let us be comforted; if we have come in fearfulness, let it vanish in trust; if we have come in hatred, purify our hearts by the touch of Thy love for all mankind, made known to us in Christ Jesus our Lord, Amen.

ANXIETY

God gave us not a spirit of fearfulness; but of power and love and discipline.

II TIMOTHY 1:7 (K.J.V.)

A GENERATION AGO it was popular in some circles to explain religion away as due to fear. Even today the theory is not entirely dead because it has the kind of easy simplicity that spares one the inconvenience of further thinking. But for most discerning people, surely, it has become ludicrous to hold that contemporary religious belief springs mainly from fears which the advancement of science has automatically made unnecessary. The exact reverse is more nearly true. Our age, having dispensed almost entirely with fear of God, now finds itself paralyzed with dread when it contemplates man and his powers; and what makes this dread so acute is precisely the loss of faith — the sense that modern civilization has gone empty at the core.

The New Testament makes it perfectly clear that fear and anxiety are supposed to be met and conquered by Christianity, instead of being exploited as a disreputable means of keeping religion alive. In the second letter to Timothy, we are told that "God gave us not a spirit of fearfulness; but of power and love and discipline." And one could go on quoting passages to the same effect from almost every book of the New Testament.

We have a right, therefore, to test a person's grasp of the Christian faith by whether his life is riddled by anxiety; and whenever we make this test we encounter an instructive difference between the glib things people say with their lips and the nervous twitchings they have in the pits of their stomachs. We have a right to measure the religious bankruptcy of our age partly in terms of what might be called "the twentieth-century jitters." We have the right to judge any version of Christianity by what it offers in attempting to meet this most vexing problem.

But a moment's reflection makes us realize that we must discriminate between legitimate and illegitimate worries. Clearly some kinds of fears are salutary and even indispensable. As one writer has put it: "In a profound sense schools spring from fear of ignorance, industry from fear of penury, medical science from fear of disease. Every saving invention . . . and every intellectual advance . . . has behind it as a part of its motivation the desire to avoid . . . some dreaded thing." *

There is such a thing, then, as failing to be afraid when we *ought* to be afraid. Refugees from countries

* Harry Emerson Fosdick, *On Being a Real Person,* Harper & Brothers, New York, 1943.

in which civil liberties have been lost tell us that one of the most insidious features of the police state is that it often strangles freedom very gradually and imperceptibly. When the peril becomes fully apparent, it is already too late to fight. In other words those who cared about liberty were not *alarmed* deeply enough and soon enough. And the United States should profit by their experience.

Often, however, our anxieties are misplaced. Our society is full of people who are terribly worried about success and prestige, but not worried half enough about what they are doing to themselves. From any sensible standpoint they ought to be bothered about the ulcers and heart attacks they are building up for themselves; they ought to be bothered about the fact that their children are strangers to them; they ought to be bothered about the fact that their friendships are superficial. No amount of money can compensate for the way they are robbing themselves and making slaves of themselves. They have every right to be anxious; but they are anxious about the wrong things.

The kind of fear that *is* legitimate goes hand in hand with sympathetic and responsible concern for human life. We can escape it only by becoming callous, or by playing the ostrich act, or by putting up a tremendous bluff. And religious faith will deepen this concern as it deepens our capacity to care about the right things. Often we run away from it, lest it break

our hearts. Often we run away from it because there
seems to be so little we can do. But in the end,
Christianity teaches us to stand fast. Learning how to
meet such fears without being overwhelmed by them
is part of the meaning of Christian suffering. A grim,
agonized awareness of human need may drive and
guide us onward, when otherwise we would falter.
And when we reach that point where we have literally done all that we can, our sense of kinship with
suffering humanity may deepen our contrition, si-
lence our accusations, and teach us our inescapable
dependence upon God.

Is it not true that the crushing events of these years
have forced some people to stop worrying about
trivial things because they have had such momentous
things staring them in the face? I know this does not
always happen, and frequently there is a hollow
sound when someone says, "Of course I ought not to
complain about my own troubles in view of the terrible things people are suffering in Europe and Asia."
Actually the person goes right on complaining about
his own troubles, and those far-away agonies do not
lessen his self-centeredness one whit. But for some, at
least, especially for some who have encountered the
very worst circumstances, new levels of understanding
and faith have been reached right in the center of
catastrophe.

How shall we explain this? Is it not clear that men
can use and transform their fears, instead of running
away from them, only when love and trust are some-

how present? The principle which Christianity embodies at this point is not arbitrary, for it rests on a law as wide as life itself. Let me cite an instance where no specifically religious connotations are involved at all. In his biography, the physician Hans Zinsser tells of how he discovered one day that he was suffering from leukemia, and therefore knew that he had only a few months to live. He goes on to describe how this knowledge awakened him suddenly to the full value of every sunrise and sunset, made him sensitive, as he had never been before, to the wonder of every living thing, to the kindness of his friends, and to the affection of his family. In the face of something he could not remedy at all, he was able to write these lines to his wife:

> Now death is merciful. He calls me hence
> Gently, with friendly soothing of my fears
> Of ugly age and feeble impotence
> And cruel disintegration of slow years.
> Nor does he leap upon me unaware
> Like some wild beast that hungers for its prey,
> But gives me kindly warning to prepare:
> Before I go, to kiss your tears away.
> How sweet the summer! And the autumn shone
> Late warmth within our hearts as in the sky,
> Ripening rich harvests that our love had sown.
> How good that 'ere the winter comes, I die.
> Then, ageless, in your heart I'll come to rest
> Serene and proud, as when you loved me best.*

This man could face death because he had found in love something stronger than the fear of death.

* Hans Zinsser, *As I Remember Him*, Little, Brown and Company, Boston, 1940.

For most of us, however, legitimate fears are not so much the end of the problem as the mere beginning. The really baffling anxieties do not broaden our sympathies, awaken us to ethical responsibility, or deepen our courageous trust. They paralyze us when we need to do our best, they make us aloof from people when we want to understand them, they throw us into fits of nervous temper when we want to be reasonable, and they fill us with a nameless, blue horror. Some of us suspect that these anxieties possess a peculiar quality which, along with television, hydrogen bombs, and supersonic speed, is an invention of the twentieth century. As Erich Fromm has put it: "Since modern man regards himself as a commodity, his security depends upon conditions beyond his control. If he is successful, he is valuable; if he is not, he is worthless. Now whenever one feels that one's own value is constituted primarily not by what he is, but by one's fate in a competitive market with ever-changing conditions, one is driven to strive slavishly for success and any setback is a disaster. Helplessness and insecurity are the result. Yet throughout the whole process of education, in the family, and from kindergarten through college, the individual is made to feel that the meaning of his life is bound up with something that can be destroyed by a mere change of fashion or a bit of bad luck."

Recent psychology has shown that the anxious person is the product of a society that insists on exploiting him, instead of respecting his value as an individual. And, interestingly enough, the anxieties are often most intense in lands like our own, which talk the loudest about respect for the individual, while following economic and social patterns that flagrantly violate the ideals we profess. Where a whole social pattern is involved, it is obvious that superficial, piecemeal methods will not accomplish much. Yet I must admit that a certain amount of contemporary preaching tries to meet the problem by precisely such methods. Ignoring the theological content of the Gospel, ignoring its ethical implications for economics and politics, the parson sets himself up as a sort of twentieth-century witch doctor, who can drive away worries by uttering happy incantations every Sunday. Actually, it does no good to tell people to stop worrying about their personalities or their jobs or their marriages, so long as their basic desires for superiority and prestige remain untouched. And the attempt to use Christian faith as a means for acquiring the kind of cheery charm that will get one to the top in this competitive scramble is about as complete a perversion of the Gospel as one could imagine.

What then does the Gospel say? It says, in effect, that individual anxiety cannot be conquered except by a basic change in our human relations and in our relationship with God. I can understand why many people today take a cynical attitude toward this answer, because it involves nothing less than an inward transformation of our society at the very core.

But I cannot see any cheap and easy answer that gives the slightest promise of really working.

The whole point of the Church, from the very beginning, has been that it is a community based on fellowship with God, whereby the community of this world is to be transformed. That implies a fellowship where persons are accepted for their own sakes instead of because of any economic, social, or racial status they may occupy. It implies a group wherein no one feels secretly helpless, because the vicious habit of judging people in terms of superiority and inferiority has been replaced by genuine comradeship. It implies a community where no one is blinded by hostility and suspicion because the fear of being exploited by others has disappeared. It implies a society where slavery to guilt and vice has been replaced by the gratitude of the forgiven man whose gratitude makes him ready to forgive others.

This is a picture of what the Christian Church ought to be, a leaven in the sodden lump of our bitter world. And I submit that it is a picture of human relationships wherein anxiety has been conquered. Some of us would fall into despair at the terrible discrepancy between this ideal picture and the Church as it actually is — if it were not for one thing. Despite all its defects, Christian fellowship has given us an actual experience of what genuine serenity and trust can mean. It has given us a taste, however fleeting, of what our text means by "power and love and discipline." And once we have actually experienced how the love of God *can* break through the vicious circle of our fears, we know that this provides the only permanent answer to the problem of anxiety.

Most gracious God, who knowest us better than we know ourselves, as we come into thy presence our disguises and defenses fall away. In the light of thy holiness and mercy we see ourselves for what we are. We acknowledge that we are anxious about the wrong things — about the attainments of others, about our own security, our own virtue, our own power.

Therefore we bring before Thee every doubt, every resentment, every secret hatred, every blind impulse, every confusion, weakness, and failure. Grant, we beseech Thee, that as we reveal our bondage, Thou wilt take our captivity captive and give Thyself unto us according to the measure of the gift of Christ. Restore us to fellowship with Thyself, that we may be made whole again as individuals and as peoples; and teach us, with new hearts and minds, to understand each other's needy cries, through Jesus Christ our Lord. Amen.

DEEP SORROW AND DEEP JOY

Fear not; for, behold, I bring you good tidings of great joy, which shall be to all people.

LUKE 2:10 (K.J.V.)

IT WOULD NOT BE DIFFICULT to prove that one of the most remarkable things about the Bible is the way in which it combines notes of deep sorrow with notes of overwhelming joy. And it does not need to be proved at all that Christ's career of suffering and sacrifice is surrounded, so to speak, by song. It begins with an event of which we sing: "Joy to the world, the Lord is come." And it ends, so far as this earth is concerned, with an event of which we sing: "Jesus Christ is risen today, Alleluia!"

Yet all of us would have some hesitation in saying that the purpose of Christianity is to bring happiness into the lives of men. The word "happiness" has been ruined by its associations with worldly comfort and self-indulgence. And the phrase "religious happiness" has been ruined by its associations with the sort of person we might call a Cheerful Cherub. The world can be going to pot around his ears, but he remains happy — or perhaps I should say "slap-happy" — because his pious cheeriness has apparently robbed him

of the ordinary human equipment for comprehend-
ing the facts of life.

Yet over against both worldliness and sentimen-
tality we need a sound conception of Christian happiness. And the Bible provides the clue by joining
deep sorrow with deep joy. Surely a capacity for these
two feelings goes together, and the person who cannot
pass through the one cannot reach the other.

Therefore, the first thing to be said about Christian
happiness is that there are no short cuts. It cannot be
aimed at directly, for it is reached only by first bringing our minds and hearts and lives into a right relationship with God. "Seek ye first the Kingdom of
God . . . and all these other things shall be added
unto you." The terrible thing about the short cuts we
follow is that when we try to reach happiness on
cheap terms, what we get as a consequence is bound
to be cheap. That is why the so-called pleasure-
seekers in any age are always the most bored and dis-
satisfied people on earth. That is why anyone who
aims directly at self-realization always turns out to be
only a fraction of a man, whereas those who truly
find themselves are always the ones who have learned
how to forget themselves.

The next thing to be noticed is that Christian happiness is reached, not by a repudiation of human desire, but by a transformation and fulfillment of it.
Too much preaching sounds to the layman as though

he must relinquish all his ordinary interests and pur-
suits in order somehow to achieve a kind of saintly
felicity. And he cannot quite picture himself in the
role. Moreover, one can hardly blame him for being a
bit skeptical, when those who preach so eloquently
about sacrifice usually manage to eat and dress toler-
ably well themselves.

The corrective is to recognize that God *has* created
man for happiness. All of our capacities for physical,
intellectual, and aesthetic satisfaction can and should
be usable in the life that He has appointed for us.
Part of the meaning of the Incarnation is that Christ
came into the world, not to save tenuous spirits, but
to save men of flesh and blood.

He comes to restore that good creation which we
have spoiled. We have taken capacities for pleasure
which could be a harmonious part of life and twisted
them into enslaving vices. We have taken powers of
imagination and intellect which could provide the
blessings of knowledge and culture, and twisted them
into instruments of misery and destruction.

Therefore a part of the Christian message to un-
happy men is that there is a real remedy for anxiety,
and lust, and hatred, and loneliness. This remedy is
applied not by turning *away* from the legitimate
satisfactions of life, but by restoring them to their
proper role.

To be sure, the remedy often calls for sacrifice — a
sacrifice of egotism, pride, and mistrust. But unless
Christianity can offer men what they *truly want* at the

end of the road of sacrifice, we can hardly blame anyone for refusing to start down that road.

Now I believe that men really want to be rescued
from their guilt; they really want to cease being
cogs in the machine of an industrial civilization that
is grinding toward doom; they really want to be able
to stand on their feet in dignity and freedom; they
really want to find a meaning in life commensurate
with the spiritual longings that lie starved within
their breasts.

It is true that there are plenty of people who act as
though they did not want these things at all. But ask
yourselves how much of their behavior is due to a
carelessness, a despair, a numbness, come upon them
precisely because of their failure to find anything that
can give them abiding satisfaction. So far as I can
see, the chief cause of sin is not selfishness — it is
emptiness.

Finally, if what I have said is true, then joy is a
legitimate test of Christian character. George Bernard
Shaw once suggested that in a properly organized society all those who commit crimes will be put in
hospitals, while those who contract common colds
will be put in jail. A similar reversal of ordinary assumptions takes place once we define salvation in
terms of openness and joy, and define damnation in
terms of isolation and rigidity.

For then we see that many people who are sincere
believers with their heads are atheists in their feel-

ings. God is alive in their creeds, but dead in their hearts. From them one might learn, perhaps, that Christ has been crucified by the world's misery and sin, but hardly that He restores to us that God-given beatitude which we have lost.

We are surrounded by many kinds of "Christmas cheer" and "Easter joy" that are mockeries. Let us not forget the God-given way whereby we may listen gladly to His "good tidings of great joy."

Lord of all might and compassion, who knowest our frame and rememberest how weak we are, memories of a distracted life rise up against us to dim the joy of thine infinite and untiring care. Have compassion on our unworthiness, we beseech Thee; because Thou delightest in mercy and willest our good always, create in us a sincere desire for whatsoever things are true, just, honorable, pure, and of good report; mold us inwardly to Thy will; so unite us with Thyself in love and confidence that whatsoever Thou bestowest we may gratefully use, whatsoever thou withholdest we may cheerfully resign, and whatsoever thou commandest we may diligently perform, though Jesus Christ our Lord. Amen.

MAN'S ISOLATION AND GOD'S
INTERVENTION

Woe to him who is alone when he falls and has not
another to lift him up.

ECCLESIASTES 4:10

At present I am learning bit by bit, but then I shall
understand, as all along I have myself been understood.

I CORINTHIANS 13:12 (Moffatt's translation)

THE AUTHOR OF ECCLESIASTES utters a complaint as
old as the human heart when he reflects gloomily
upon the fate of the solitary individual. He depicts for
us how men must make their lonely way amidst op-
pressions without a comforter; how they strive to build
a place of security by ambitious labor, and all they
earn for their trouble is the envy of their neighbors;
how they try to satisfy themselves with riches, and yet
not all the gold in the world can compensate for the
human relationships they have missed along the way.
And the only consolation he can offer us, apparently,
is that we may make the most of companionship.

To be sure, men are untrustworthy. They approach
each other with watchfulness and suspicion; like beasts
of the jungle, they are always ready to draw back in an
instant and bare their fangs. But in so far as the bar-

riers which separate men from each other can be broken through, companionship is the only tangible remedy for an otherwise hopeless isolation. "Woe to him that is alone when he falleth, and hath not another to lift him up."

Contemporary literature and philosophy remind us that man has not gotten over his sense of solitude. We hear much, for example, about our insignificance amidst the cosmic immensities, although I am inclined to think that this is a bit sentimental. The problem is spiritual, not quantitative; and we could perfectly well put up with the fact that our solar system is a third-rate affair, we could even put up with the brevity of our days upon earth, if we had some sense that our hopes and despairs, our joys and sorrows, our loves and hates, were not in the end shut up within the impenetrable privacy of our own souls.

Surely one of the greatest shocks in personal development comes at that moment when a man has discovered himself sufficiently to realize that he is incurably alone. One day he finds that his family is strangely rent asunder by the impassable gulf that yawns between youth and age. His parents are still understanding, perhaps; but they belong to one generation, he to another; and they have forgotten what it is like to be young. Or the world in which the pattern of his future life seemed so securely fixed is shattered by the realization that not all the strong, sober people he knows put together can guarantee him a job, or his liberties, or his prospects for happiness, or safeguards against misery, injustice, and war.

These things may happen suddenly or slowly, painfully or calmly; but however they happen, this second birth into responsibility is at the same time an entrance into a solitary citadel which a man can never leave again. And much of the lust for power, much of the greed and sensuality in human life, is due to the anxiety that tortures us within those citadels. Since we are the sole defenders, we must make them impregnable against the attacks of circumstance and the hostility of other people. We become, as the saying goes, the sort of person whom one never really gets to know.

It is the fate of modern man to live in a kind of world which intensifies this feeling of isolation. The feeling has always plagued our race; but there have been times when it was alleviated by the presence of a stable society within a stable universe. Modern man has paid a fearful price for his excess of individual freedom. For he has shifted the burden of supporting the moral structure of history from the shoulders of providence to his own shoulders. As Mr. Walter Lippmann, has written: "Having cut the individual off from the traditions of the past, modern secularism has left man in isolation. It has left him to make his uprooted and incoherent way through a struggle in which there is no principle of order. To struggle alone is more than this isolated individual can endure; and so he gives up his freedom and his

priceless heritage. Because he has forgotten the religion which puts human life in an eternal perspective, he cannot withstand the fanatical forces which
destroy freedom for the sake of national and racial
solidarity."

In other words, this spiritual isolation is a sort of
practical atheism which every one of us carries around
in his heart; and it is far more to be dreaded than the
pallid skepticism of intellectuals in a classroom. For
this practical atheism issues in fantastic hopes and un-
restrained self-assertion in the effort to throw a cloak
over despair. This is the Nemesis which dogs the foot-
steps of godlessness; and our own day has brought
forth incarnations of this Nemesis so terrible that we
can no longer be blind to it. Modern man has tried
to be an unyielding Atlas, who could sustain alone
the world that his own ideals had fashioned. But he
made the mistake of thinking that this self-worship
would take beautiful instead of devilish forms. He
forgot that when loneliness and misery and despair
finally break through to bitter expression, men prefer
worshipping blood, race, and soil in the fellowship of
a faceless mob to worshipping a lonely ideal in a cosmic vacuum. From the standpoint of a religious interpretation of history, totalitarianism is the result of
practical atheism within the hearts of desperate men;
having lost all hope of positive blessedness, they have
found fellowship in nihilism. Man is created for community; and even when he shuts himself off from God,
he still seeks community in desperate and inverted

ways. Man cannot stand isolation because he was not meant for isolation.

The Christian Gospel speaks directly to that isolated man who dwells within the heart of every one of us. For its message is this: that although solitude may be the last word so far as we are concerned, it is not the last word so far as God is concerned. Although we may shut ourselves off from God, God will not leave us alone. Man has to come to terms with His Creator, either through the agony of estrangement or through faith in Christ's reconciling love; but twist and turn as he may, man cannot really escape into isolation.

> Whither shall I go from Thy Spirit?
> Or whither shall I flee from thy presence?
> If I ascend up into heaven thou art there;
> If I make my bed in Sheol, behold, thou art there.
> If I take the wings of the morning
> And dwell in the uttermost parts of the sea;
> Even there shall thy hand lead me,
> And thy right hand shall hold me.
>
> PSALM 139:7–10 (K.J.V.)

This is our faith and our confidence; this is the sense of companionship which girds us when all trust in men has betrayed us; this is our hope of fellowship while fellowship is being destroyed on every side. And yet, there are moments of dark night when the feeling of alienation from God seems too strong for us. After all, we are part of this contemporary world, and how can we feel anything but that God is poles asunder from such a world? We have made our bed in hell, all right; but how can we add: Behold, thou art there?

We need not look beyond the 13th chapter of First Corinthians for the Christian answer to such questions. Dr. Moffatt translates verse 12. "At present I am learning bit by bit; but then I shall understand, as all along I have myself been understood."

St. Paul's statement means that if we could know the whole truth that knowledge would be the same thing as having perfect fellowship with God. But we know only in part; there is the difficulty. This faith that there is one who knows us all along, and whom we shall meet face to face on the other side of death, is a faith which all the evidence of experience and all the efforts of rational thought can only partially vindicate.

Indeed, most of the instances in recent years where our partial knowledge has been extended have only plunged us more deeply into dismay. We can certainly say of our outlook during these past decades that we saw only in a riddle; but the full implications of the kind of a world we are living in, as they have overwhelmed one nation after another which hoped to remain shielded from their impact, have only deepened the riddle. We know now that there is no sense in trying to avoid the truth; but we still cannot see how knowing the truth holds out much promise of making us free. We were blind, not because we wanted to shut ourselves off from God, but because we wanted to shut ourselves off from facts too baffling to endure.

One might put it this way: The only way we could see of maintaining belief in God was to hope against hope that human good will and intelligence would somehow bring forth spiritual resources more powerful than those forces which were hurling us headlong toward catastrophe. And much of the irrelevance of our religious thinking was due to lack of genuine faith that we could understand God's will best by a deeper penetration into unpleasant facts. Unconsciously we feared that if we learned the whole truth we would be brought face to face, not with God, but with the dead end of a meaningless thoroughfare.

Now we know that if the world still rests within the overruling power and providence of God; if there is a moral structure in history, demanding that men shall organize their lives on the basis of fellowship and love; if human wickedness cannot defeat God and cannot violate His will with impunity; if all this is true, then it is a truth which lies beyond our present comprehension. It is something which we see only darkly through the riddle of contemporary events. But one thing is clear. If we can ever see God face to face, it will only be by going *through* the wasteland of these facts which we tried so long to avoid.

Most men have to be shocked into an awareness of tragedies and evils of whose depths they had no adequate inkling. We throw a protective covering around our minds to ward off the slings and arrows of outrageous fortune. A time-honored technique for stilling the uneasy voices which rise up when we see the miseries of the underprivileged, or the victims of racial intolerance, has always been to point out the complexities of the problem and the impersonal working of economic machinery for which no one is responsible. You remember the dispossessed sharecropper in *The Grapes of Wrath* who started out to get revenge on whoever had thrown him off his land. He found out that the agent was only carrying out the orders of the local bank; and that the bank president was responsible to a head office in New York; and that the New York office was responsible to investors who had never heard of this sharecropper. And so, in the end, there was no one to shoot. Everyone was responsible to somebody else; but nobody was responsible for his misfortune. Now of course the complexities of such a situation are factual; but there is a vast difference between whether the facts are used to put conscience to sleep or whether they stab it into wakefulness.

Our imaginations are so limited that the needs and experiences of others can hardly take on vividness and concreteness until we find ourselves in a similar predicament. I remember during the air raids on London, the fearful sense of unreality we attached to the raids while we sat in safety in New York and tried to picture what was happening. We had to think of specific friends or specific places in order to gain any comprehension at all; but we still felt abysmally deficient in understanding. It was not until there were some false air raid alarms in New York that some of us

vaguely began to apprehend in the viscera, instead
of just in the brain, what war means to a population.

The point is that we should have to be different
sorts of people from what we are in order to be able
to understand the plight of our fellows more clearly.
Is it any wonder, then, that we know only in part?
We would have to be different sorts of people, surely,
in order to understand fully how God's justice and
mercy are working through the events of our own
times. "All things work together for good to them that
love God." (Romans 8:28, K.J.V.) Yes; to them that
love God. And we need only look within ourselves
and out upon our world to realize why we cannot see
all things working together for good.

As Christians we hold that man's isolation is not
final. We hold that God, who knows our sinfulness
through and through, has nevertheless opened the
way to fellowship through forgiveness in Christ. But
we hold these things by a faith which goes far beyond
our partial knowledge.

Still, partial knowledge is not just sheer ignorance;
and perhaps we can say with St. Paul that we are
"learning bit by bit." Some things have laid hold on
us in our present situation with an urgency which
makes our previous assent to them merely lip service
by comparison. We may always have said that no pre-
tences avail in the sight of God. We may have said
that there is an eternal Spirit who knows the worst
and the best about us all along. But we have learned

a great deal about how this works out concretely in both dread and comfort.

Take the lies of political propagandists, for example. Does not their frantic character attest to the fact that the truth cannot be completely stilled even within the breast of the most insensate human being? The truth will not down. Someone, somewhere, knows this propagandist all along for the liar that he is; and this angers him. The frenzy with which he throws himself into self-justification shows that at some level of his being there are still the vestiges of an honest man. He may have done his utmost to shut himself off from the truth but the truth will not let him alone.

Or take our own disposition to refuse any responsibility for events which are beyond our individual power to prevent. We have tried to isolate ourselves from the collective nature of guilt. We have been inclined to say: "We Christians do not want war; we will do all in our power to avert it. So if war comes, it is not really our fault. And all those other naughty people who are to blame will discover that no one wins a war any more than anyone could win an earthquake." But present circumstances make all arguments about whether we are responsible for what is beyond our individual control academic. We cannot abstract ourselves from history. Now we know, in part at least, the solidarity of our guilt. We know the tragedy of being accountable for what we cannot prevent, because we are caught up in the same situation as all the other peoples who do not want war and find themselves unable to prevent it. The myth of our American moral superiority is dead. We are "learning bit by bit."

Finally, we know enough to realize the contrast between any form of human solidarity and fellowship with God. When we are threatened by spiritual isolation, we are not duped into believing, with the writer of Ecclesiastes, that human association provides the only protection we can expect to find. Indeed, one of the issues which is being fought out in today's international struggle is whether the state, in default of God, shall be regarded as the supreme object of man's loyalty and devotion. And no matter what attitude we take toward participation in a war, whether cold or hot, surely all Christians can unite in the faith that beyond the riddles we cannot solve, beyond the guilt we cannot escape, beyond the sin and ignorance that hem us in, we are called into the fellowship of One who understands us all along. No matter what suffering or sorrow may lie ahead, He has been there before us, and He waits for us at the end.

Almighty and most merciful God, we thank thee that through the gift of thine only begotten Son Thou hast made us know that we are not alone because Thou, our Father, art with us. And though we walk through the valley of the shadow of death, we shall fear no evil, for Thou art with us. Be Thou our Comforter and Guide, we beseech Thee, now and forever. Amen.

THE GRANDEUR AND MISERY OF MAN

And behold, they brought to him a paralytic, lying on his bed; and when Jesus saw their faith he said to the paralytic, "Take heart, my son; your sins are forgiven." And behold, some of the scribes said to themselves, "This man is blaspheming." But Jesus, knowing their thoughts, said, "Why do you think evil in your hearts? For which is easier, to say, 'Your sins are forgiven,' or to say, 'Rise and walk'? But that you may know that the Son of man has authority on earth to forgive sins" — he then said to the paralytic — "Rise, take up your bed and go home." And he rose and went home.

MATTHEW 9:2–7

IN THE SEVENTEENTH CENTURY, Pascal wrote: "Christianity is strange. It bids man recognize that he is vile, even abominable; and bids him desire to be like God. Without such a counterpoise, this dignity would make him horribly vain, or this humiliation would make him terribly abject." *

Pascal was a highly educated man, one of the greatest physicists and writers of his day; yet in the twentieth century most educated people would reject his saying on both counts. In the first place, they do not like the notion that man is vile. And in the second

* *Pensées,* Modern Library Inc., New York, p. 171.

place, they cannot take seriously the idea that man should desire to be like God.

So from the perspective of many educated people today, Christianity looks not only strange, but also contradictory. And we can easily imagine an enlightened professor saying to Pascal: "Make up your mind. Either wallow in your morbid teaching about man's wickedness, or dream your mystical dreams about his eternal spirit. But by all that is sane and sensible, don't try to have it both ways at once."

Let us begin by examining this modern refusal to admit that man is vile, As we all know, the real substitute for Christianity today, inside as well as outside of the Churches, is confidence in human possibilities. We encounter its widespread influence in various forms. The most familiar version is faith in technological progress and in the power of science to control nature and human affairs. Sometimes, however, the stress falls on man's capacity to achieve gracious living through artistic creativity and culture. And sometimes confidence is placed in the ability of the lonely individual to win through to integrity despite surrounding social evils, family maladjustments, and the stupid pressures of the mob mind.

In any event, a Christian has a strange experience when he enters into a debate with this modern faith in man. At the outset he usually finds himself in the unenviable position of being regarded as an anachronism. He is a curious survival from an earlier age when people tried to explain things by referring to invisible, supernatural powers. By contrast, his opponent in the debate seems to be a person who has his feet planted firmly on the earth. His opponent knows that everything must be understood in terms of natural forces which can be observed, classified, and controlled.

But as the discussion continues, a reversal gradually takes place; and before long it turns out that the Christian is the iconoclast. He is the one who is asking hardheaded, embarrassing questions about whether the facts of history adequately support this faith in human possibilities. He finds these up-to-date hopes staggeringly out-of-date. Yes, it is the Christian who is now accused of robbing men of the confidence they need. He is the annoying Devil's Advocate who insists that the pleasant side of the facts has been exaggerated and the unpleasant side minimized. He is the not-so-tame cynic who tells modern men that they have been cherishing outworn illusions.

Let me explain, as best I can, *why* this shift occurs in the debate. Having lost the "counterpoise" of which Pascal speaks, modern thinking is compelled to say two opposite things which cannot be held together. On the one hand, it has to declare that the evils which man commits are not really his fault. On the other hand, it has to cling to the hope that man can save himself, because it has nothing else in which to place its hopes.

Now if you are interested in contradictions, I suggest that you ponder this one. Man is so much at the mercy of temporary ignorance, mass social forces, and his own endocrine glands that he is primarily the *vic-*

tim of evil rather than the *doer* of it. And yet man — this *same* man — is thought to be capable of so directing his resources that eventually he will construct a just and stable civilization, if only he can learn how to trust himself instead of relying on God.

Is it any wonder that contemporary Christian thought has sometimes been driven into excess as it tries to put a stick of dynamite under this mountain of wishful thinking? Yet instead of excess, what is really called for is counterpoise. I see no reason why the Church should not make common cause with all scientists, artists, and humanitarians who are struggling for justice and freedom, so long as it retains clarity about its own conception of human nature. For then it will always know that *the responsibility whereby man may contribute to his own salvation is inseparable from the responsibility whereby man is the author of his own follies.* It is the modern view which splits man apart into an innocent automaton and a potential "godlet." It is the Christian view which sees man as a unity — a responsible, sinful, child of God. From the latter standpoint it is impossible to become blind to man's vileness without at the same time becoming blind to his grandeur.

This fact comes out with special clarity in connection with the way each person is caught in the collective evils of our time. Think for a moment of how the refusal of national governments to admit guilt continually prevents the discovery of a mutual basis for co-operation. Of course nearly everybody realizes that the East and the West are like two paranoids who sit barking at each other in a mental hospital. But how many of our contemporaries are able to recognize that in the last analysis the disease springs from a religious defect? The missing factor in the whole picture is contrition. Each side is quite right in thinking that any concession would be seized upon as a sign of weakness; each side is quite right in thinking that any gesture of good will would be only a gesture. But all this is true because we, as peoples, have lost touch with the strength of genuine repentance; all this is true because we have lost touch with that dreadful courage which enables us to look at our own policies in the light of righteousness instead of merely in the light of expediency. I submit that a greater readiness on the part of each country to acknowledge its own *vileness* in the sphere of international relations would introduce a greater measure of the *dignity* of man into the sphere of international relations.

In the passage above from the Gospel of Matthew, the paralytic gets up and walks only *after* his sins are forgiven. Our world is like that. It does no good to tell men that they should forget their guilt, when they are riddled by it. And we shall remain paralyzed in our efforts to move toward trust and understanding until the full seriousness of our own involvement in evil can come out into the open and be acknowledged. To be sure, one part of the problem of guilt arises at that point where an individual blames himself unduly for things that are really the fault of society; and because the Church is concerned to place responsibility where it belongs, the cure of souls must always be directed toward rescuing the individual from a slavery that society has imposed upon him. But the other part of the problem of guilt arises at that point where a man's sharpest insight tells him that he is not wholly blameless. He sees his own hatreds and fears, and he knows that these qualities, writ large, spell injustice and war. To tell him then that he has no need for forgiveness is to ask him to lie to himself. At that moment, to stifle his prayer for healing is to stifle the moral dignity which makes him fully human.

Yes. Christianity is strange. For its refusal to give up the word "sin" is a blessing in disguise. Its real motive in bidding man to recognize that he is vile is a humane motive. Only by recognizing the evil in ourselves, can we learn compassion for others. Only by joining with others in a confession of need, can we find forgiveness and strength. It is as though we must first be made brothers in mutual contrition, before we can become brothers in mutual trust.

But now we must turn to the other half of Pascal's statement. Without the strange counterpoise of Christianity, man's dignity makes him horribly vain.

Once again, many educated people today would deny this flatly. They claim that by getting rid of God we can eradicate all the fantasies by which man has tried to picture himself as destined for eternity. By learning that he is a child of nature, and nothing more, man will supposedly enter into true humility and true mastery. He will become humble, because he will realize that his life is of no cosmic importance. And he will become masterful, because he will subjugate nature in the service of humane ends.

At the first session of the Constitutional Convention, when someone suggested that the meeting be opened with prayer, Alexander Hamilton is reputed to have said, "We have no need of alien influences." That, I daresay, is one of the most extreme expressions of American isolationism on record. And this attitude is reflected in thousands of our contemporaries who literally feel no need for desiring to be like God. Why, they ask, should we look to any such alien influence for guidance? God is supposedly eternal. Then how can He know what it is like to be a mortal man who must make his way through time? God is supposedly Spirit. Then how can He know of the joys and sorrows of a life which is bound up with the body? And last but not least, who wants to be perfect anyway? It is a static, impractical, *boring* notion.

As a corrective against religious sentimentalism, this modern protest has real value. But it needs to be pointed out that our age has not avoided delusions of grandeur by getting rid of God. On the contrary, it has shown very clearly that when men stop worshipping God, they often begin to play God themselves in one way or another. Perhaps you have heard the story of how a certain tycoon once said to Dr. Joseph Parker: "I'm a self-made man, you know." And Dr. Parker replied: "Sir, you have lifted a heavy burden of responsibility from the shoulders of the Almighty." Of course the point is that no man is suited to take over such a responsibility. But when we lose the counterpoise which holds our gifts in perspective, we forget the difference between desiring to be *like* God and desiring to *be* God. At its worst, this means that the twentieth century finds itself worshipping at the shrine of some leader, some party, some system, where men claim fanatically that they can do no wrong.

Against such a background the Christian gospel seems strange indeed, because it attaches the greatness of man not to the dimension of power, but to the dimension of tragedy. I have no desire to minimize the amount of harm which results from a frustration of natural impulses; but it seems to me that much of the emptiness of modern life comes from a different kind of frustration. It results from the loss of a clear vision of what man was meant to be — in terms of blessedness, and sacrifice, and eternal significance. We are being stifled by an outlook which makes us cogs in a machine. We find no vision commensurate with our own longings for spiritual freedom because we have lost touch with the meaning of tragedy.

In a recent novel one of the characters says: "We spend our life in chains; but our right to cast off our chains, and to learn from our bondage — that is the point. The right to tragedy. That is what I mean by freedom. It is the trivial-minded, mechanical man who is incapable of tragedy. Tragedy occurs only to free

men; to men who live on the crest of life and who refuse to accept regimentation or defeat. It is the medal
which fate pins on the breast of the fallen hero; it is
the final acknowledgment of man's dignity." *

And so, to those who have renounced God because
He is eternal, the Christian Gospel tells a story of one
who was a mortal man and who made His way through
time. To those who have renounced God because He
is pure Spirit, the Gospel tells of One who knew the
temptations and sufferings of human life. And right
there it bestows the strange counterpoise which gives
us a perspective on ourselves. For in Christ we are
made aware of the misery of man when separated from
God, and the grandeur of man when restored to God.

Admittedly, when we look at mankind in the mass,
what we see is not very magnificent. But if we will
adopt Pascal's vantage point we can discern in each
individual a person for whom Christ died — a person
destined to wander in chains until his capacities for
freedom, honesty, and love have been released by that
figure on the cross. Then we can speak with boldness
of the dignity and grandeur of man.

*Almighty God, awaken in us, we beseech Thee, a de-
sire to find Thee, that we may find ourselves; and lead
us, by the pathway of perfect service into the blessedness of perfect freedom, through Christ our Lord.
Amen.*

* Frederic Prokosch, *Age of Thunder,* Harper & Brothers,
New York, 1945.

JUDGING OTHERS

Judge not, that you be not judged.

MATTHEW 7:1

TAKEN OUT OF CONTEXT, these words seem to sanction an attitude of moral indifference. They seem to imply that since we are never perfect, we have no right to use our critical faculties at all. They seem to forbid every protest against wrong and all discernment of evil in others.

But when we look more closely, we discover that the saying is really asserting *the universal inescapability of moral law*. Jesus is declaring that when we pass judgments on others, the same standards apply to ourselves. And when we take Him seriously, our consciences are immediately startled into full wakefulness instead of being lulled into indiscriminate tolerance. To be sure, we are forestalled from being hasty and offhand in hurling condemnations at others; but this is because we are made to realize that they may come back, like a boomerang, and strike us.

Hans Zinsser tells the story of a great Norwegian scientist who was disturbed by the fact that the old captain of a fishing ship he was on was careless about

keeping the log. When the meticulous scientist re-
proached him, the old captain replied:

"You are a professor, and I am a captain. I have lived
a long time, and I have seen many things. I tell you —
and you can remember it — the truth can be exaggerated, Professor."

There is no time when we are more likely to feel that
the truth has been exaggerated than when some of our
most penetrating ethical judgments are applied to ourselves.

No doubt man's capacity for self-transcendence is a
wonderful thing; but like most wonderful things about
us, it is also perilous. It can give rise to the illusion that
by condemning egotism and ruthlessness and compla-
cency long enough and hard enough, we can somehow
lift ourselves completely above them. The words of
Jesus bring us back to earth with a thud; for they make
us realize that God alone is in a position to judge mankind from any such eminence. They make us realize
that conscience begins by saying "Thou art the man,"
and only afterward can it be trusted to turn its gaze out-
ward toward others.

This does not abolish our condemnation of economic injustice; but it puts the whole matter in a new
light when we begin with our own privileges. It does
not abolish our condemnation of war criminals; but it
places the whole matter in a sobering light when we
apply our definitions of crimes against humanity first
to the deeds of our own nation. And the terrible thing
is that, since every insight can be abused, a minister

may so easily fall into the convenient strategy of beginning with his own confession of sin . . . merely as a convenient strategy.

But there is no escaping from the fact that everyone stands revealed and judged by the spirit in which he praises and condemns. And all too often what we censure most severely in others are the very faults in ourselves which we are most anxious to ignore.

There *is* a kind of tolerance in our Lord's saying, then. But it does not arise from moral indifference. It arises rather from the fact that only one who recognizes his own faults can honestly include himself under the standards by which he judges others. For example, one of the reasons why Alcoholics Anonymous has had such success is that its members are in a position to take a truly discerning attitude. Obviously they are not indifferent about the problem, because they know its seriousness better than anyone else. But instead of standing off at a distance, they can take their places alongside the man who is in the midst of the struggle. In other words, they have hit upon the truth that all the moral fervor and righteous indignation in the world cannot help another person unless we take our place alongside him, where the judgment that we pronounce falls on both of us.

And yet this is not quite the last word. For once we have felt to the full the inescapability of moral judgment — only then, and not before — we realize that God has also dealt with us in another way. It is only through a conviction of sin and need that we ever get

into a position to understand the love of God. So it
is false to talk as though His love skipped over morality. But any man who has once faced his own shortcomings realizes that in the most profound sense God has
not simply passed a scrupulous judgment upon him.
No. In Christ, He has taken His place along side us,
instead of standing afar off in condemnation. In Christ,
God has taken upon Himself the consequences of His
own moral order and the sin of mankind. It is in this
sense, and this sense alone, that we can repeat White-
head's words when he says that "love is oblivious to
morals."

But any man who has felt the life-giving presence of
Christ alongside him in moments of deepest remorse
and failure can no longer be primarily interested in
passing easy judgment on others. Knowing how God
looks upon the penitent man, he will pray for the
power to do likewise.

So it is that the Christian Gospel takes right and
wrong up into itself; and, without abolishing them, it
transmutes them by suffering into a new disposition of
the heart, where a new kind of life begins.

Henri Barbusse tells of a conversation overhead during the last war in a dugout full of wounded men. One
of them knows that he is dying, and he says to the other:
"Listen, Dominique, you've led a bad life. There are
no convictions against me. There's nothing on the
books against my name. Take my name. Take my life.
I give it to you. Straight off, you've no more convictions. Take it. It's there in my pocketbook. Go on, take

it, and hand yours over to me — so that I can carry all your crimes away with me." *

At an infinitely higher level this is what God says to the human race through Christ: "Take my life. I give it to you . . . And hand your life over to me, so that I can carry all your sins away."

Almighty and most gracious God, teach us, we beseech Thee, to see all men as Thy children whom our Lord has died to save. Make us ready in our judgments to be guided by Thy righteous will, and make us eager, in our forgiveness, to reflect Thy merciful love, through Jesus Christ our Lord. Amen.

* Henri Barbusse, *Under Fire*, Everyman's Library, E. P. Dutton & Co., Inc., New York, 1928.

MAKING FRIENDS WITH TIME

And I gave my heart to seek and search out by wisdom
concerning all things that are done under heaven: this
sore travail hath God given to the sons of man to be ex-
ercised therewith. I have seen all the works that are done
under the sun; and, behold, all is vanity and vexation of
spirit. . . . Therefore I hated life; because the work
that is wrought under the sun is grievous unto me . . .
Wherefore I perceive that there is nothing better, than
that a man should rejoice in his own works; for that
is his portion . . .

ECCLESIASTES 1:13–14; 2:17; 3:22 (K.J.V.)

I have fought the good fight, I have finished the race,
I have kept the faith.

2 TIMOTHY 4:7

THESE SCRIPTURAL PASSAGES offer contrasting descrip-
tions of what might be called "the wisdom of maturity."

The author of Ecclesiastes, having seen everything
and tried everything, finds that life is caught in a
wearisome circle from which there is no escape. The
best solution he can offer is that a man should rejoice
in his own works. He tells us that we had better find
joy in what we can get out of life as it goes along, and at
some time or other, every human being suspects that

157

this advice is right. No one has a monopoly on the idea that history is an endless cycle of birth and death. Every man, as he realizes his bondage to time, feels the familiar complaint pass through his mind. No one, for example, can truthfully deny that at some level he resents the fact of death. You find the universe quite unimaginable when you try to think of it without *you* in it to discern comic, tragic, and humdrum things in precisely the way that you alone can discern comic, tragic, and humdrum things.

Therefore, we should be grateful to the author of Ecclesiastes because he tells us the full truth concerning the outcome of his wisdom. On the surface, he makes a very sensible adjustment. He does not try to run away; he accepts the passing moment; he does not cry, like a child, for something more. But underneath, the full truth comes out when he says: "Therefore I hated life." Despite his maturity, his honesty, and his wisdom, he is left at the end in despair.

When we encounter the utterly different ideas of St. Paul, it is as though our own voices were speaking within us, from another part of ourselves. Every man knows what it is to fall into despair. Every man also knows what it means to yearn for a sense of completion. No one fears the bare fact of mortality half as much as he dreads the possibility that his life may turn out to be a wasted mockery, a sort of ghastly caricature of the man he might have been. Everyone longs, in one way or another, to be able to say: "I have fought the good fight, I have finished the race, I have kept the faith."

Note therefore that this contrast between emptiness and fullness, between despair and trust, reflects the difference between having to be satisfied with our own works and being able to place our final confidence in God's work. It is no accident that the man who can say: "I have fought the good fight," has long ago lost interest in his own works for their own sake. "Not I, but Christ" runs like an antiphonal refrain throughout his thinking.

Of course the problem of how to dispose of time so that it will yield a sense of fulfillment, instead of a sense of emptiness, is as old as the human race. But the problem takes special forms in our day. This is partly because we try so hard to convince ourselves that we can find all we need in a purely temporal existence. And it is partly because the *lie* on which these efforts are based is becoming harder and harder to conceal.

For example, the medical benefits which are lengthening the span of life mean that more and more people are going to have to wonder about what to do with old age. Unless some catastrophe intervenes, we shall become a group of elderly persons who are either running things, or who are annoyed because we are not running things. Yet as Christians we should know that longevity in itself, as a technological improvement of the twentieth century, solves absolutely nothing. If life is empty, then eighty years of emptiness can only be regarded as twice as vacuous as forty years of emptiness.

Once when I was a small boy on a journey with my parents, I stayed up late on the train because we were scheduled to cross the Mississippi at midnight. I had read about the great river in my geography and history books, and I was tremendously excited at the prospect of seeing it for the first time. So despite my sleepiness, I kept my eyes open. Finally as the train rushed across the bridge, I could dimly see a quiet, flat expanse in the starlight. But when my parents said: "There, you've seen the Mississippi," I felt vaguely cheated. Somehow it seemed to me that there should have been something much more grand than a few glimpses of sluggish water in the darkness.

For many people the transition from youth into age is something like that experience. They go forward through the preparatory stages with excited anticipation, confident that they are approaching something magnificent; but, passing quickly over the mainstream, they suddenly find themselves on the other side. And they too feel vaguely cheated. They have reached and passed what they were trying to stay awake for, and they say to themselves: "Surely that can't be all there is to it. There ought to be something more."

What does this mean? It means that beyond physical and psychological problems, the mature person faces the spiritual problem of believing that life can go forward in meaning, instead of receding from it. Our society has tried to solve this problem by looking exclusively toward the temporal future. If a man cannot reach the great goal in his own life, then perhaps at least his children, or his nation, or the institutions he serves, can reach it. But I hardly need stress the fact that this solution is becoming increasingly ineffectual.

For one thing, it does not work very well even for young people. We can hardly exaggerate the moral and spiritual consequences for youth which result from the fact that planning carefully for old age and a fully rounded life does not make much sense any more. Twenty years ago a friend of mine wrote a poem to his son and entitled it: "Be kind to the old man you're going to be." The poem impressed me then, but I could not blame a college boy today for feeling that it was irrelevant. Young people have always found it hard to believe that they would become old. But *our* young people have exceptionally good grounds for doubting whether any decisions should be based upon such a remote and precarious prospect.

Yet looking exclusively to the temporal future is even *less* adequate as a solution of the spiritual problems of later life. We need not draw up a list of gifted and useful people who have broken down in moral collapse, or insanity, or suicide. Even among those who retain their positions, their health, and their reputations, we can sense the ravages of an invisible malady.

Some time ago *The New York Times* carried an article about a scientist who declared that doctors should learn how to treat the shock of realizing that "one is growing old," just as effectively as they treat any other kind of shock. One of the methods proposed was to adopt the approach of "Chinese sages and poets [who] taught that happiness is to be found in tranquillity, moderation . . . and aesthetic appreciation of the little things in life." Now I wonder how a doctor can expect to transfuse the tranquillity of an ancient culture into a retired American businessman with high blood pressure. I also wonder whether in any case the Chinese method produces an adequate solution.

The really shocking fact is something man knows all along, although toward the latter part of life the full impact of the fact begins to catch up with him. *The really shocking fact is that any possible arrangement of temporal goals and satisfactions leaves us with a sense of incompleteness.* All life is a groping for the recovery of something lost, and a groping for the fulfillment of something eternally new. If man is fashioned for fellowship with One whose creative power reaches back behind all beginnings and out beyond all endings, then we can see why the incompleteness of temporal life shocks and baffles and grieves us. But then this nostalgia of the soul cannot be cured by any wisdom, Chinese or otherwise, which counsels us to be content with our lot as children of nature and mortality. Indeed, if man *is* only a child of time, then being shocked at the simplest and most obvious evidence of our linkage to time is a very curious and unaccountable disease.

From the Christian standpoint the crucial problem of maturity is how to move forward toward spiritual freedom instead of settling down into a case of hardening of the spiritual arteries. The fact that the scope of one's choices becomes narrower in certain respects causes no misgivings so long as the doors we pass through lead us into mansions larger than those we could have entered otherwise. Any man who has found a vocation commensurate with his hope of eternal life does not complain over the other careers he might have pursued. Anyone who has discovered how a marriage can make time serve something timeless would regard it as ludicrous to lament over the many splendid members of the opposite sex who must be passed by in order to be monogamous. In short, the narrowing of alternatives as life advances is designed to make possible the deepening and enrichment of spiritual freedom.

For that very reason, however, the most perilous turning point in life often comes, not in youth, but in middle age. The powers, skills, and ambitions which occupy the center of attention during the earlier years will no longer suffice. Unless *fruition* can begin to set in, then strain and stagnation are sure to do so. We can understand why youth always says: "Just give us a little time." But sooner or later the law of diminishing returns begins to operate unless we can turn toward things that are not merely "futuristic" but are "eternal" in their worth. The older man who has nothing but the perpetuation of his youthful achievements to keep him going is bound to feel that existence is becoming faded and outworn. He may increase his income, his power, and his authority. But spiritually he becomes a man with a promising future behind him.

In trying to describe this perilous turning point I should like to draw a distinction between having a *fixed* character and having a *formed* character. I once heard of a signpost in the California desert which well illustrates what I mean by a *fixed* character. The sign said: "Choose your rut carefully; you will be in it for the next thirty miles." Frankly, one of the things that frightens me about so many middle-aged people is that they are incapable of bringing really fresh thought to bear upon the great problems of our day. Perhaps I feel keenly about this because I have recently been in Europe. It is staggering to come back to this country and find that many of those who talk most about individualism are completely indistinguishable from their neighbors. In a train or at a dinner party all one has to do is touch upon a sensitive topic such as anti-Semitism, Negroes, labor, taxes, or Russia, and then sit back for the long recital. It is like putting a nickel in a jukebox. I do not deny that sometimes one hears opinions that are true and sensible, or at least understandable. What disturbs me is that even the truths have become so automatic, so familiar, so threadbare. No price in fresh thinking and insight has been paid in reaching them. And so the speaker sitting before you ceases to be a real individual; he changes before your hypnotized gaze into a type, whose personality, clothes, automobile, brains, and wife are completely interchangeable with thousands of others of his type.

I am making a plea for a genuine return to "American individualism," therefore, when I say that this fixity of character is a tragedy. It is a tragedy because it deprives us of the wisdom and flexibility which might otherwise be furnished by these able, successful people.

If the true remedy is to be found in a *formed* character, then we urgently need to examine what that implies. The sort of person I have in mind will indeed have a dependable scale of values and a definite sense of purpose, but he will bring them to bear upon each new situation with freshness and openness. One may not be able to predict how he will react, but one must be able to say of him: "I can trust his integrity, even though the way he meets a new problem may surprise me."

As he grows older this person realizes that the disappointments, injustices, and tragedies of life are less remediable than young men can ever admit. He realizes that age needs forgiveness even more than youth because the sins of age become increasingly ingrained and unrecognized. He realizes that passing years leave less chance of requiting old wrongs, less chance of making radical departures. And nevertheless life becomes increasingly rich and meaningful for him because he is in touch with a wisdom higher than man's. His life is in touch with a divine life which gives stability to his purposes, and yet leads forever onward toward one increasing purpose.

The most striking fact about such maturity, it seems to me, is that no one can reach it by aiming at it directly. Reflect for a moment and you will agree that many of the most significant aspects of your experience were entered into unawares. In some instances they may have seemed quite trivial at the time. In other cases, you could not bless the painful gift which broke you open, because you could not realize then that it would enable you to grow.

We know that the man who sets himself to capture happiness by storm is foredoomed to failure, and that genuine happiness comes as a by-product of self-forgetfulness. We should know also that no man can really conquer time by trying to rejoice in his own works. Precisely because he could not see beyond trying to "get a lot out of life" for himself, the author of Ecclesiastes was finally driven into a hatred of life.

But if St. Paul is right, then it is possible to make friends with time. We cannot do so directly, by loving the significance we can impose upon it. We can do so only indirectly, by learning to love the Eternal. Then we believe that God can continue His work of making us new creatures to the end of our days. And in an age when men have turned their "itching ears" toward fables, we are left with plenty to do. The secret of staying spiritually alive is, quite simply, to care more about truth, and love, and forgiveness, than about what happens to us. And in so far as Christ enables us to live this way, we know as much about eternal life as men can; for we know the sufficiency of God, here and now. And surely it is the sufficiency of God, here and now, for each stage of life, on which is based the Christian hope of immortality.

O God, our heavenly Father, whose gift is length of days, help us to make the noblest use of mind and body throughout all our years. Grant us new ties of friendship, new opportunities of service, joy in the growth of children, sympathy with all who are in need, and blessedness in communion with Thee. Keep us from pride and outgrown ways, from blindness that will not see the need for change, and from impatient judgments toward those who differ from us. Take away all fear of death, and all despair or undue love of self, that with glad hearts we may follow Thy will for us, through Jesus Christ our Lord. Amen.

A CHRISTIAN SENSE OF DIRECTION

He steadfastly set his face to go to Jerusalem.

LUKE 9:51 (K.J.V.)

IN HIS BOOK, *Wind, Sand and Stars,* Saint-Exupéry tells of being lost in an airplane over the Sahara at night:

"Suddenly, when already we were in despair, low on the horizon a brilliant point of light was unveiled on our port bow. A wave of joy went through me . . . It could not but be the beacon of an airport, for after dark the whole Sahara goes black and forms a great dead expanse. That light twinkled for a space — and then went out! We had been steering for a star which was visible for a few minutes only, just before setting on the horizon between the layer of fog and the clouds.

"Then other stars took up the game, and with a sort of dogged hope we set our course for each of them in turn. Each time that a light lingered a while, we performed the same crucial experiment . . . And despite our dwindling fuel we continued to nibble at the golden bait which each time seemed more surely the true light of a beacon, was each time a promise of a landing and of life — and we had each time to change our star.

"And with that we knew ourselves to be lost in interplanetary space among a thousand inaccessible planets, we who sought only the one veritable planet, our own, that planet on which alone we should find our familiar country-side, the houses of our friends, our treasures." *

I take this incident as a symbol of the spiritual predicament in which a great many of us find ourselves today. We feel lost, as though we were flying through space over a dark expanse, without any sense of direction. And in our desperation we pin our hopes upon the guidance of one beckoning light after another. But amidst the confusion of competing aims and ideals we cannot find our way back to earth, back to our proper spiritual home, where we shall have solid ground beneath our feet once again, amidst friends and familiar surroundings.

First of all, we are tempted to pin our faith on *things* — on possessions and external accomplishments. In the midst of a war, when a nation is fighting for its very existence, it is natural and inevitable that immediate military and political goals should occupy most of our attention and energy. But many people in such a situation seem almost glad to be so busy with these immediate tasks that they do not have time to look ahead. It is a relief to be so busy saving civilization that they have no time to ask what they are trying to save it for. And

* From *Wind, Sand and Stars,* copyright, 1939, by Antoine de Saint-Exupéry. Reprinted by permission of Harcourt, Brace and Company, Inc.

there are far too many among us whose real guiding star throughout the conflict, when they think about the matter at all, is still a materialistic one. Their visions of victory are composed largely of shiny automobiles, glass-brick houses, air-conditioning, helicopters, and maintenance of the highest standard of living in the world.

Is the terrible sacrifice of a war worthwhile if from it we return to a life of enslavement to externals? You and I have seen the strait jacket of our "American Way of life" fasten its grip upon our friends. We have seen them gradually kill spontaneity and imagination for the sake of forcing themselves into the narrow patterns of success. They become "well-adjusted" to the community: that means occupying a certain income bracket, having safe political opinions, and having not more than two children. They look back upon their earlier days, before the zippers on the strait jacket had begun to pin them down, as a time of foolish dreams. Actually those were days when they were still alive. They have "arrived" now; but in the process they have somehow lost themselves.

There are some who will stubbornly persist in following this false star. And we can understand why. When they feel themselves lost in space, without any clear sense of direction, they try to drown the feeling by pretending that possessions, prestige, a mastery of external circumstances, are the aims of their lives. But it does not take much discernment to see that such people are really lost and groping. They have spent all

their time seeking security, and they have failed —
as the lines of worry on their brows and the ulcers in
their stomachs make very clear. And their failure is
really an encouraging fact. For as it drives them fever-
ishly from one task to another and from one amuse-
ment to another, it shows that no man can reach genuine satisfaction or serenity so long as he stakes his
life on *things,* and lets his spirit starve.

But there is another, and a more beguiling star,
which may also lead us astray. For it is terribly lonely,
trying to find one's way amidst darkness — like Saint-
Exupéry over the Sahara. And no man likes the loneliness of having to take responsibility for his own life.

There is a story about a party which was crossing
a salt desert on its way to California. Nerves became
raw and a fight broke out over some trivial matter.
And then the leader invoked the terrible law of the
desert: "If you cause trouble, you will be forced to
go it alone."

No man wants to be forced to "go it alone." We
can understand why all of us are tempted to seek a
sense of security and a sense of direction by *going
along with the crowd.*

Obviously there are some respects in which social
conformity is simply good sense. But I should like to
call attention to its dangers. Think of how many of
our most important convictions are reached by mass
reaction instead of through independent judgment.
Think of how easy it is today to figure out all of a

man's opinions merely by locating one of his major prejudices. All you have to do is prick him where he hates the Jews, or hates the Negroes, or hates labor, and the rest follows, like poison flowing from an open wound. And the point is that these are fear reactions. They arise in a man because he feels lost. Not knowing how to find his way in a world of rapid social changes, he gains a false sense of security by finding some scapegoat, someone whom he can blame.

This is not just a matter of ignorance. You can find plenty of college graduates and Ph.Ds who have no more critical perspective upon their own fear reactions than other people. Give them five or ten years away from the campus and they simply reflect the mass opinions of *their* profession, *their* stratum of society, *their* section of the country, *their* friends, and *their* favorite journalist.

Now most of us are not entirely to blame for this, because there is a long history behind our lack of self-reliance. All of us have to begin as children in dependence upon parents and other guides who quite properly take care of us and lay down certain conditions which we must follow.

But an arrangement that is normal for childhood becomes disastrous if the process of growth is stopped. What we then see is a case of arrested development. We see a person who has so fallen into the habit of having his beliefs and decisions furnished for him by other people that he has never learned responsibility. Then take that person, place him in the presence of some great social wrong or some serious temptation, and what does he do? He looks around to find out what others will think or say. Like a chameleon, he takes his color from the surrounding environment. He says: "Well, if so-and-so does it, it must be all right for me to do it." Thus conscience begins to get passed around from one neighbor to the next. And after awhile we get so used to the crying evils and injustices surrounding us that we come to regard them as something natural and normal.

Surely this unthinking, mass reaction is one of the things we are fighting against today in our struggle with totalitarian forces. Surely, if we are concerned for a new birth of freedom, that also means we are concerned for a new birth of the individual conscience, rising above the hatreds and prejudices which sweep across the world like angry torrents. And none of us can find a true sense of direction unless he is able, if need be, to stand alone against these tides. Very well then; instead of fixing our gaze on things, or on popular opinion, let us learn to look *within* for steadfastness, *within* for a sense of direction. But wait a moment! Is that not the point at which our confusion becomes greatest? Is that not the point where we find the cause of the whole trouble, instead of the remedy? We would never follow false stars unless there were something wrong inside ourselves. We look within and we find a mass of conflicting impulses — a tug-of-war going on between good and bad motives.

Half the time we feel defiant, ready to justify our-selves fiercely in the sight of God and man. And the other half of the time we feel weak and disgusted; we wonder how we can be so stupid, so impulsive, and so selfish.

What good does it do to tell us to look inside? It is the last thing we want to do. What we see then is entirely too discouraging. If you think this picture is exaggerated, ask yourself whether there is anyone — anyone in the wide world — to whom you would be willing to tell the whole, unvarnished truth about your own life, without leaving anything out.

No, we cannot worship ourselves. We cannot live on our own substance. We cannot find a true light to steer by within our own hearts; they are too dark, too confused, for that.

You know the story of how Noel Coward once sent a picture post card of Venus de Milo to a little girl, and wrote across the bottom: "This is what will hap-pen to you, if you don't stop biting your finger nails." Well, the same sort of thing happens to us when we try to live entirely on our own resources.

Where, then, can we look for a sense of direction? Think for a moment of what it would mean to possess that mysterious equilibrium which enables a man to move through triumph and tragedy without deviating to the right or to the left. Think of a steadfastness of purpose which lifts a man above the crowd, with its wayward shifts of enthusiasm. One day they shout in triumph and strew the streets with palms; a few days later they cry: "Crucify Him! crucify Him!" But whether they are for Him or against Him, this man knows what He is about. And make no mistake, it often takes as much courage to keep one's head in a moment of popular acclaim as in a moment of persecution and anguish. A man has to have a clear sense of direction if, in the hour of victory, he casts prudence aside and throws the money changers out of the Temple.

We ask for guidance, for steadfastness, for something that will give meaning to our lives — for some true beacon which will lead us back to our proper spiritual home. And as we think of that Figure, let us remember it was no accident that He could put aside all thought of possessions and prestige; it was no accident that He could bring the inner resources of a steadfast soul to the events which He encountered. He brought to life a sense of direction which finally led — to a Cross.

But in His lonely integrity He was not really alone. The secret of His power is, after all, an open secret. His source of strength is available to every one of us if we have the courage to look at material possessions, and human society, and the innermost secrets of our own souls in the clear light which God sheds upon them.

When we stand in His presence, we *cannot* make an idol of material things, we *cannot* be complacent about social evils, we *cannot* be blind to our own terrible faults. But He does not guide us by some distant vision. Instead, He enables us to see this familiar world with clear eyes. Like Saint-Exupéry's one true beacon, He leads us back to earth.

Mark Twain tells in one of his books of how the Mississippi River cut through a narrow neck of land one night, so that a Negro who went to sleep in Missouri woke up to find that the land he lived on was now east of the river; and since that made it part of Illinois, it made him a free man.

The same sort of thing happens to anyone who penitently asks God for strength and forgiveness. He awakens to the same familiar earth, the same people, the same self. And yet everything is wonderfully different, because he stands up as a free man.

Merciful Father, who willest not that thy children should wander in darkness; pour the light of thy Spirit into our minds and hearts, that we may discover what is thy holy will, and discern the true from the false, the evil from the good, that we may henceforth walk in all humility in the paths of heavenly wisdom and peace, to the glory of thy holy name. Amen.

WHAT LIES AHEAD

We hear that some of you are living in idleness, mere busybodies, not doing any work. Now such persons we command and exhort in the Lord Jesus Christ to do their work in quietness and to earn their own living.

II Thessalonians 3:11–12

For the mystery of iniquity doth already work; only he who now letteth will let, until he be taken out of the way. And then shall that Wicked be revealed, whom the Lord shall consume with the spirit of his mouth, and shall destroy with the brightness of his coming . . .

II Thessalonians 2:7–8 (K.J.V.)

For now we live, if you stand fast in the Lord.

I Thessalonians 3:8

Our generation is able to listen with fresh attentiveness to those passages in the New Testament which speak about the end of history. We can understand their urgency for we also carry on our activities with a haunting sense that time may be running out. And we can understand their sharp clarity; for most of the desires and ambitions which seem to be important when an indefinite number of years stretch ahead turn out to be petty and worthless when seen in the white light of eternity.

Now can you imagine a more complete and shattering revolution in human thought? The habit of planning in terms of an endless historical process has been one of the distinguishing characteristics of modern man. Our self-esteem has depended largely on being able to regard ourselves as the bridge between a stirring past and a magnificent future. We recognize that this method of promoting self-esteem is no longer plausible; and yet we hardly know what view of life to put in its place.

Such circumstances, I say, have removed the cotton from our ears so that we can really listen when the New Testament speaks about the end of history. For some, this has meant a new sobriety, a new earnestness; the old glibness and self-assurance are gone. For others, it has meant a kind of shrieking defiance, a desperate clinging to those enlightened, modern hopes which have become so pitifully blind and antiquated.

I am sorry to say that most of the recent attempts to retain faith in man make me feel very old. They might have seemed timely a generation ago. But today they are obviously an ostrich act; and one can imagine the ostrich muttering something in the sand about sweetness and light, onward and upward forever, at the very moment when disaster strikes his exposed posterior.

We must acknowledge, of course, that much contemporary Christian thought has also been guilty of refusing to face facts, so that perhaps it ill behooves us to make unkind remarks about our secular neighbors. Indeed, until recently our whole age has been unable to realize that having to come to terms with eternity is "normal" for men. It seems so foreign to our make-up that we either run away from it entirely or embrace it in startling, exaggerated forms.

But if you will examine what St. Paul writes to the Thessalonians, I think you will agree that he, at least, is exempt from such charges. He was writing to this Christian community in the earnest expectation that the end of the world was near at hand. We forget that he could not see his missionary endeavors in the perspective of the ensuing centuries when Christianity would spread across the world. Unconsciously we assume that he knew what he was starting. We picture him as knowing that this little band of Thessalonians would be the forerunners of men who would incorporate Greek philosophy and culture into the great tradition of Christianity. We say to ourselves: "He had good reason for wanting to tidy up their pagan morals. He had good reason for worrying about whether, after only a brief acquaintance with the Gospel, they could stand up under persecution. Look how much depends upon it. Why, unless his Gentile mission succeeds, Christianity won't spread through the Mediterranean world at all. And, of course, it simply has to. Otherwise, where will we be in the twentieth century?" So we see St. Paul as one striving to win his battle because the future is depending on him.

Needless to say, nothing of this sort was in his mind at all. And it is appropriate in a world like ours that we should scrutinize his attitude toward Christian work and responsibility at a time when he thought that the end of everything might be just around the corner.

We can confine ourselves to three observations taken almost at random from these letters. The first is this. "We hear that some of you are living in idleness, mere busybodies, not doing any work." Our first impulse, of course, is to admire St. Paul's common sense when he admonishes such people. And yet it is easy for our approval to spring from a kind of activism which is very far from his intentions. Certainly he did not imagine that by their daily tasks men could do much either to hasten or to postpone the day of judgment.

How different our own attitude has been. We are in favor of work because we assume that thereby we can determine our own destiny. In the presence of obstacles and perils it is a good American custom for everyone to get together and "do something." Until very recently this habit has in a sense paid dividends. But now we realize that the ills of the world cannot be removed merely by shouting, whether prayerfully or profanely: "For God's sake, why doesn't somebody *do* something?"

We know that we are in for an indefinite period of delicate economic, political, and military decisions; but we also know that these activities are not enough.

We know that a radical change must occur within the heart of man himself — a radical change which cannot be brought about by any of our familiar methods of organization, marketing, and efficiency.

Yet am I wrong in thinking that most people today, having put their trust for so long in these familiar methods, are almost incapable of appreciating the religious transformation which has always been at the very center of Christianity? Either they try to forget their fears by keeping so busy that they will not have time to think about them; or they throw up their hands in despair and see no sense in trying to do anything.

To both types St. Paul says: "Even though you cannot hasten or delay the coming of God's Kingdom, the best way to prepare for it is through faithfulness in each day's tasks." A generation ago many Christians felt that if man really cannot bring in the Kingdom, then the logical consequence is to do nothing. Like the Thessalonian loafers, they felt that we should let God do the worrying. But today we are better able to appreciate the meaning of St. Paul's words. It is this. Christianity offers a unique kind of serenity to men and women. If we will acknowledge our tragic limitations as well as our undeniable potentialities; if we will acknowledge especially our dependence upon saving power greater than our own strength of will; then we can face life with a new freedom and a new effectiveness. Let me put it in plain English. If you are going to die tomorrow, the best way to spend today lies not in bitterness or terror, but in integrity and trust. It is possible in any moment — even the last moment — to possess the kind of fidelity to Christian love and its tasks which time cannot destroy. This is a Christian kind of "living in the present" which is at the opposite pole from selfish "living for the moment."

Men who face death discover that the precious things which come to mind in moments of peril are homely and unspectacular. They remember untroubled hours spent with friends. They remember their loved ones. They remember special moments which dropped unexpectedly into their daily lives, and which, when one looks back on them, seem like gracious gifts from heaven. And they know that it is only through entering into daily life as it comes — its joys and miseries, its accomplishments and frustrations — that one can ever be ready for eternity.

What I am trying to suggest is that it is quite possible to feel the need for religious trust and still be a man of action. Throughout history, the great believers have at the same time performed mighty deeds. But they have been rescued from the tyranny and feverishness of mere activism, because they have been able to look beyond their own success or failure to the providence and mercy of God.

The second thing St. Paul says to the Thessalonians is that the final accounting with evil still lies ahead of them. He speaks of a "mystery of iniquity" which is at work in the world. He declares that Roman law, at best, can hold it in check for a while, underneath the surface; but evil is bound to break loose again and to lead mankind toward destruction by means of strong delusions. This wickedness will not finally be overthrown except by the power of Christ.

Surely the applicability of these words is too obvious to need much emphasis. We know that the final accounting with evil still lies ahead. Instruments of law and order can at best hold this beast in check for a while. But just to make sure that you do not misunderstand, let me say quite plainly that I am not trying to twist the Apostle's words so as to make them apply to Russian Communism. The mystery of iniquity lies ready to break forth in any part of the world — including the United States of America. What St. Paul saw so clearly is that man is *always* in this situation. The *final* accounting with evil always lies ahead, so long as history lasts.

Therefore the final solution — beyond immediate plans and contingencies — comes only as the issue is squarely joined between this mystery of iniquity, which destroys man, and the power of Christ, which can save him. That issue is being joined now within the hearts of this generation. And St. Paul's words speak to us as though he foresaw our situation: "This is no time to lie down and wait for the end. The final battle, the final test, lies ahead of you. Make ready for it." And he concludes his warning with this sentence: "Therefore stand fast and hold the traditions which ye have been taught."

That leads directly to a final observation from these letters. It has to do with Christian solidarity. Let me remind you again that the Apostle's concern for the unity of the church does not spring from a strategy for spreading Christianity down through the centuries. He views the fellowship of men in Christ as a foretaste in time of the Eternity which is soon to come upon them.

Now I happen to believe that in cold, realistic, practical terms, the best hope for world civilization lies in the Christian Church. Despite its divisions, its stuffiness, its slowness, its enslavement to nationalistic prejudices, social conservatism, and rigid dogma; the Church is mankind's most effective instrument for opening channels of understanding, for restoring mutual confidence, for instilling contrition, for allaying anxiety, and for opposing fanatical will-to-power. To a generation groping for some world-wide basis for justice, we *must* say: "A world society already exists. It *is* possible for men to find a loyalty which takes precedence over everything that divides them into warring groups. It *is* possible for men to relinquish their own narrow interests for the sake of a community which surmounts distinctions of race, nation, and class. That loyalty and that community are found where men are drawn together in the worship of Jesus Christ."

Yet, important as all this is, we must admit that
from St. Paul's perspective, it turns out to be sec-
ondary. No matter what happens in the future — no
matter whether there *is* a future — the solidarity of
men and women in Christian fellowship is the most
precious thing in the world.

Nothing could make this plainer than the words
he uses in the third chapter of the first Epistle. There
he writes: "For now *we* live, if you stand fast in the
Lord." This is strange language for an apostle to use
in addressing a group of fairly shaky converts, who
were recently pagans. One might well assume that St.
Paul could be confident of his own spiritual security,
whether this little band of followers remained faithful
or not. But no. His conception of the organic unity of
the Church is such that wherever Christians falter,
he dies a little; and wherever they stand fast, he
breathes again.

Which one of us can foresee exactly what will befall
our world in the days that lie ahead? Amidst such
ignorance we may be ready to recognize that men have
always had to confront eternity, and we may be grateful for anything that removes our peculiarly modern
unreadiness to do so. Yet I for one could not rest content, even with the knowledge that God can enable
a man to meet each day's task as it comes. I could not
rest content with the further knowledge that a crucial
battle for the allegiance of the hearts of men, against
staggering forces of evil, still lies ahead. Only the last
word brings us to a full reconciliation. For it means

that no one of us is left to himself, in life or in death. Each man must stand fast for himself; but wherever he does so, others live through him. Each man is left free and responsible in his faith; and yet, by that faith itself, he is bound by invisible, supporting ties; and bound to the needs and sympathies of every man who seeks for God amidst the fellowship of human tragedy and the community of human trust.

Almighty God our Father, teach us so to live that each day's task may be a preparation for eternity. Make us ready, through trust in Thee, for whatever struggles and sorrows lie ahead. And draw all men toward that fellowship which may unite us as heirs of Thy grace and servants of Thy will, through Jesus Christ our Lord. Amen.